Birdlife at Chincoteague

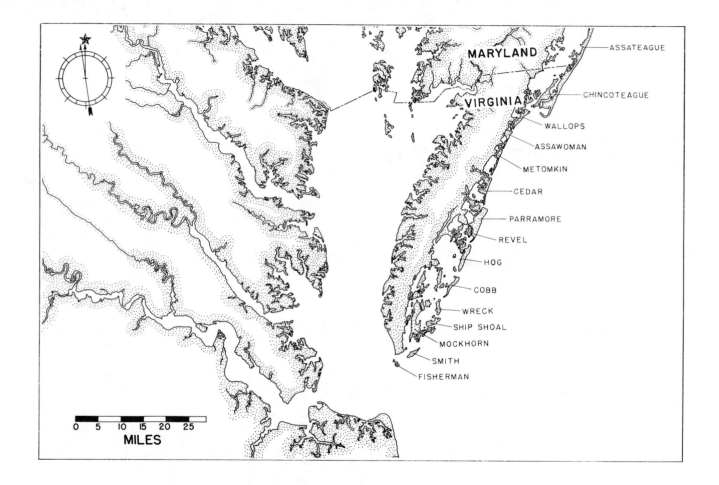

Birdlife
at Chincoteague

and the Virginia Barrier Islands

Brooke Meanley

TIDEWATER PUBLISHERS CENTREVILLE, MARYLAND

Library of Congress Cataloging-in-Publication Data

Meanley, Brooke.
    Birdlife at Chincoteague and the Virginia barrier islands.

    Bibliography: p.
    Includes index.
    1. Birds—Virginia—Chincoteague Island. 2. Birds—Virginia.
    I. Title.
QL684.V8M42   598.29752'21   79-27187
ISBN 0-87033-257-0

Manufactured in the United States of America

First edition, 1981; fourth printing, 1994

Front cover photograph: Marion Glaspey,
    Wetlands Institute

Back cover photograph: Mike Haramis, USFWS

Contents

Snow geese resting in salt meadow on Assateague Island in January. Dusky-colored immatures in center.

Acknowledgments

I wish to thank the following friends who supplied information, photographs, and/or drawings: Gorman M. Bond, John H. Buckalew, Danny Bystrak, Luther Goldman, S.A. Grimes, Mike Haramis, Bob Hines, Kathy Klimkiewicz, Matt Perry, John W. Taylor, Francis Uhler, and the U.S. Fish and Wildlife Service.

Thanks also to Robert Arbib, editor of *American Birds*, a publication of the National Audubon Society, for permission to publish the Christmas Bird Count data for Chincoteague and Cape Charles.

I am indebted to my wife, Anna G. Meanley, who kindly reviewed the manuscript.

Photographs are by the author, unless otherwise credited.

Brooke Meanley

The osprey obviously choose from a wide variety of nest sites. In more isolated areas it often builds its nest on the ground.

Introduction

The 70-mile chain of largely. uninhabited sea islands along the Eastern Shore of Virginia is one of the last remaining natural seashore areas along the Atlantic Coast. These barrier islands and bordering marshlands exist today pretty much as they must have in pristine times. Because of the wilderness aspect, diversity, and location of the area, they have the richest assortment of birdlife in the Middle Atlantic States.

The establishment of the Chincoteague National Wildlife Refuge in the 1940s, and subsequent acquisition of most of the chain of islands by conservation interests, has contributed immeasureably to the preservation of birdlife along this section of the coast. Thirteen of the eighteen barrier islands south of Assateague were recently acquired by the Nature Conservancy, a private conservation group dedicated to the preservation of natural areas; and in 1979 these islands were designated a national natural landmark by the Department of the Interior. The Conservancy's holdings along this section of the coast comprise 33,000 acres, known as the Virginia Coast Reserve.

Shorebirds, (Fig. 1), seabirds, (Fig. 2), and marsh birds abound, and even in the middle of winter nearly 200 species can be counted between the Maryland line and the tip end of the Delmarva Peninsula at Cape Charles. The Eastern Shore coast is known for its numerous nesting colonies of terns, skimmers, laughing gulls, herons, egrets, and ibises; large breeding clapper rail populations; large concentrations of migratory birds of various species and for the large segment of the Atlantic brant and greater snow goose populations which winter here.

Ornithologists have been attracted to the Virginia Barrier Islands since the latter part of the 1800s. In earlier years, Cobb's Island was the focal point for investigations

Fig. 1—Dowitcher (left) and knot, photographed in the summer of 1936; one of the first wildlife pictures taken by the author along the Delmarva Coast.

Fig. 2—Little (formerly least) tern chick on barrier beach a few miles south of Chincoteague, June 14, 1978.

by museum ornithologists and other professional naturalists who had a special interest in colonial nesting seabirds. Among the earliest naturalists to visit the island were Harry Bach Bailey in 1875 and Frank M. Chapman in 1902. The many ornithologists that followed in the next twenty-five years probably visited Cobb's Island as a result of the published reports of Bailey and Chapman. Several chapters in Chapman's book, *Camps and Cruises of an Ornithologist*, (1) relating to his adventures on that island and a habitat group of mounted birds in the American Museum of Natural History in New York City, where Chapman was curator of birds, are based on the sea- and shorebird nesting colonies at Cobb's Island.

George Shiras, 3rd, a former U.S. Congressman and one of North America's pioneer wildlife photographers and bird protectionists, visited the barrier islands of the Eastern Shore of Virginia in 1894 and several years following. He made an interesting series of photographs of shorebirds, clapper rails, and other birds and their nests at Revel's Island, illustrating several chapters of his two-volume work, *Hunting Wild Life with Camera and Flashlight*, published by the National Geographic Society (2).

Talbot Denmead, a biologist with the U.S. Biological Survey who visited the barrier islands in the early 1900s, told me of seeing a pile of 500 laughing gull eggs gathered by an "egger" (local term for people who collected eggs for food) near Oyster, Virginia. At that time, also, the spring shooting of shorebirds was widely practiced along the chain of barrier islands. When Frank Chapman visited Cobb's Island in July, 1902, he was told of 2,800 least terns being killed in three days and shipped to New York City to adorn ladies' hats. Laws were eventually enacted outlawing these practices.

Other ornithologists who visited Cobb's Island in the "early days" and published their findings were A.C. Bent in 1907, A.B. Howell in 1909, J.F. and R. Kuerzi in 1929, Oliver L. Austin, Jr., in 1931, and O.S. Pettingill, Jr., in 1933.

In the late 1930s, John Buckalew, second manager of the Chincoteague National Wildlife Refuge, began banding colonial nesting birds in the area. As of the late 1970s, he was still banding terns, gulls, herons, egrets and other colonial nesters, and during most of the year operated a songbird banding station in his backyard near Wallop's Island.

Other active workers in the area in more recent times have been Robert E. Stewart of the U.S. Fish and Wildlife Service, who conducted ecological studies of breeding clapper rail populations at Chincoteague in the early 1950s; Frederic R. Scott of Richmond, leader of the annual Christmas Bird Count at Chincoteague, and a principal cooperator in the Kiptopeke Banding Station where thousands of migrating songbirds are banded each fall; Mitchell Byrd, professor at William and Mary College, who with some of his students has been surveying osprey and colonial breeding bird populations; Willet T. Van Velzen and John Weske of the U.S. Fish and Wildlife Service, and R.D. Benedict who have banded thousands of royal terns at Fisherman's and nearby islands. Among other active birders presently reporting rare and unusual birds along the Virginia Coastal Strand are R.L. Ake, J.C. Appel, Philip and Paul Dumont, Charles Vaughn, and Bill Williams.

—Brooke Meanley

Fig. 3—Barrier beach bordering the ocean at Metomkin Island.

Bird Distribution in Relation to the Physiography of the Coastal Strand

The coastal strand of the Eastern Shore of Virginia is made up of a chain of barrier islands (Fig. 3) bordered on one side by the ocean and the other by salt marshes (Fig. 4), and separated from the mainland by embayments. This region of diverse and strategically located habitats lying along the Atlantic Flyway, with a north-south trending shoreline to guide birds in their travels, and with relatively moderate temperatures that keep the embayments open in most winters, is a concentration area for more than 200 species of transient birds (shorebirds, waterfowl, songbirds, others), a breeding ground for more than 100 species of birds. Most notable of these are sea-

1

birds (terns, skimmers, gulls), large waders (herons, egrets, ibises), and marsh nesters (rails, gulls, sparrows, etc.); and a wintering area for at least 30 species of waterfowl. The number of species seen on the one-day Christmas Count each year at Chincoteague and Cape Charles averages about 150 and 170, respectively. The narrow strip of land funneling birds along the coastal strand, the open waters, and abundance of food account for the high numbers of birds on the Christmas Counts at these two stations, exceeding those in the Chesapeake Bay area and at any of the 20 or so stations in other sections of Virginia.

Average January temperatures at Norfolk (just across the mouth of Chesapeake Bay from Cape Charles), at Richmond (at the Fall Line), and at Lexington, Virginia (in

Fig. 4—Salt marsh at low tide in summer. The pure stand of salt-marsh cordgrass (*Spartina alterniflora*) is typical of most of the marshlands along the coastal strand. Shrubs at right are high-tide bush (*Iva frutescens*).

the Appalachian region), are 42.4, 39.1, and 34.2 degrees respectively. There are growing seasons at these three locations of 242, 218, and 178 days.

I can recall in the 1940s seeing a patch of cotton growing on the Eastern Shore of Virginia, and also visiting an area near Eastville that had an acre or more of trees covered with Spanish moss. There is also a station for live oak, another southern specialty, on the Eastern Shore. Loblolly pine, principal tree of the barrier islands, reaches its northern limit on the Delmarva Peninsula—Delaware, the Eastern Shore of Maryland, and the Eastern Shore of Virginia.

Several species of birds are at or near the northern limit of their breeding range on the Eastern Shore of Virginia. At the northern outpost of their range in eastern Virginia, or at some point along the coastal section of the Delmarva Peninsula, are the royal tern, gull-billed tern, Sandwich tern (Fig. 5), Wilson's plover, chuck-will's-widow, brown-headed nuthatch, and white ibis. In 1977, the white ibis was found breeding for the first time in Virginia. Its nest was in a mixed heronry at Fisherman's Island located near Cape Charles. This is an extension of their breeding range northward from the North Carolina coast. The boat-tailed grackle is also a common southern bird along the Delmarva coast, with a few reaching southern New Jersey.

Species near the southern limit of their breeding range include the horned lark, tree swallow, great black-backed gull, and herring gull. Both of the gulls are much more abundant during the breeding season along the North Atlantic Coast, from New England northward. The Virginia colonies are somewhat outliers or disjunct colonies, but also a recent extension of breeding range.

Nesting colonies of these two large gulls among those of terns, skimmers, and laughing gulls bodes no good for these smaller species. An increase in the nesting populations of these large gulls that sometimes prey on eggs and young of other seabirds poses an additional hazard to nesting colonies in the egg and chick stage that often are destroyed by flood tides.

There are a dozen or more habitats extending from the littoral or immediate offshore zone across the barrier islands, salt marshes and embayments to the edge of the mainland. Some species of birds occur in several habitats, others in only one. The brown-headed nuthatch is an example of a species that occurs in only one habitat, the loblolly pine forest; and the clapper rail occurs only in salt marshes and their edge bordering the tidal guts; while the American oystercatcher nests on a bare spot in a salt marsh, on the seabeach, and along the edge of a heronry located on a spoil island in the bay and feeds in tidal guts, the shallows of embayments, in tidal pools of the salt marshes, and at the edge of the surf on the barrier beach. Laughing gulls nest mainly in the salt marsh, but forage in a wide variety of places; and the fish crow and boat-tailed grackle are highly adaptable species that probably utilize more habitats (except for nesting) in their daily peregrinations than most other species of birds of the coastal strand.

3

Kirke A. King, USFWS

Principal breeding or nesting habitats of birds of the coastal strand are the more isolated or uninhabited beaches, particularly those that lie south of Assateague Island; the salt marshes; natural and spoil islands (Fig. 6) located mainly in the embayments; and the pinewoods.

The colonial nesting common, royal, least (or little) and gull-billed terns and the black skimmers, and the individual nesting Wilson's and piping plovers are species especially associated with the sandy-oystershell-pebble-strewn seabeaches. Occasionally one of the terns or plovers will nest on a sand dune. The sand dunes are a nesting habitat of several "land" birds, including the nighthawk and horned lark; and near Ocean City, Maryland, a chuck-will's-widow, a species that usually nests in the pinewoods, was found nesting on a sand dune!

Forster's terns, laughing gulls, and herring gulls are colonial nesting birds of the salt marshes. Nesting colonies of laughing gulls sometimes number 5,000 pairs of adults. Breeding clapper rails or "Marsh Hens," willets, and seaside and sharp-tailed sparrows also are species typically associated with the salt marshes.

Fig. 5—The Sandwich tern, uncommon to rare in this area, is a southern bird that reaches its northern limit along the Virginia coast. A few pairs sometimes nest among royal tern colonies on Fisherman's Island.

Fig. 6—Typical habitat of the black duck along the edge
of Assateague Bay at the north end of Chincoteague Island.
Black ducks feed and loaf in the cove and nest
in bordering salt-marsh grass, or under nearby bushes, June 3, 1977.

Herons, egrets, and ibises, sometimes referred to as large waders, do most of their feeding in pools in salt marshes (and such places as freshwater impoundments at Chincoteague National Wildlife Refuge), but nest in mixed species colonies in cedar trees or pines on uninhabited barrier islands, and in low shrubby growth, mostly of high-tide bushes on small spoil islands. Species in this group usually include the great, snowy, and cattle egrets, Louisiana, little blue and black-crowned night herons, and glossy ibis. In some colonies, boat-tailed grackles nest in the bushes along with the large waders; and where suitable habitat exists around the periphery of these crowded shrub-covered islands, a few pairs of American oystercatchers, laughing gulls, clapper rails, and willets will also nest.

Among the breeding birds closely associated with the loblolly pine-woods habitat are the brown-headed nuthatch, pine warbler, summer tanager, chuck-will's-widow, and fish crow. In general the breeding bird fauna of the barrier island pinewoods is the same as that of the nearby mainland; and in addition to those species mentioned, would include the mourning dove, wood pewee, chipping sparrow, mockingbird, and others.

The greatest variety of birds appear during spring and fall migration, which should more appropriately be referred to as northward and southward migration, as some birds begin migrating up the coast in late winter, and many birds are moving south along the Virginia Coastal Strand in the "dead of summer." Some of the waterfowl that winter along the Virginia coast begin migrating north in February. The main northward movement of shorebirds is in April, May, and early June; with the main southward movement of these birds being in July, August, and September. The resident terns and laughing gulls, species so commonly identified with the Virginia coast during the summer-half of the year are gone by fall, mostly to wintering grounds in tropical seas of the Caribbean and coastal South America.

The migration of land birds, and especially songbirds, is much heavier in the fall than in spring. During the period of spring migration, the bulk of the songbirds of the Atlantic Flyway migrate farther inland, or from the Chesapeake Bay area and the Appalachians northward. The fall or southward migration is a little later than that of most of the shorebirds, with a peak around the first of October.

In the fall perhaps the birder's most anticipated land bird is the peregrine falcon. This endangered species migrates close to the coast, usually moving southward above the beaches and sand dunes. Its main flight is during the first two weeks in October. A close relative, the merlin or pigeon hawk, also becoming less numerous, follows somewhat the same migration path on its trip south.

With the passing of most of the fall transients in October and November, come the winter residents, most notably the waterfowl. The Atlantic brant, a small goose, and the greater snow goose, whose entire populations winter along the Middle Atlantic Coast as far south as North Carolina, have come from High Arctic nesting grounds. These two species of geese and the oldsquaw, a duck, nest farther north than any other species of birds in the world.

The geese are associated with the coastal embayments and salt marshes, the snow goose feeding largely on salt marsh cordgrass and other marsh grasses; and the brant on eelgrass, a submerged aquatic, and sea lettuce and other algae.

The littoral zone just off the beach, and perhaps a mile beyond, is an important wintering habitat of the sea ducks, the three species of scoters, the oldsquaw, two species of eiders, and the harlequin duck. Gulls of several species are associated with this habitat at all seasons. In winter the herring, ring-billed, great black-backed, and Bonapart's gulls are present; though rarely the glaucous and Iceland gulls from the far North.

Pelagic or oceanic species usually found farther at sea, but which occasionally wander shoreward or are blown in by storms, include the gannet, pomarine and parasitic jaegers, shearwaters, skuas, kittiwakes, and phalaropes.

Beyond the range of the shore-based 30-power spotting scope, there are a host of oceanic species. From a boat far out at sea one might even see a yellow-nosed albatross like the one reported some 60 miles off the coast of Delmarva on February 1, 1975 (3).

Mike Haramis, USFWS

The Atlantic Brant

There are two varieties or subspecies of brant in North America, Atlantic and black. The Atlantic brant (*Branta bernicla hrota*), (Fig. 7), is an eastern bird that nests in the Eastern Arctic, and winters mainly along the Middle Atlantic Coast. The black brant (*Branta bernicla nigrescens*) nests farther west along the Arctic Slope, wintering on the Pacific Coast of North America. The generic name *Branta* supposedly means burnt, in reference to the bird's sooty plumage. The specific name *bernicla* is

Fig. 7—Brant feeding on algae along water's edge at Chincoteague, January, 1978.

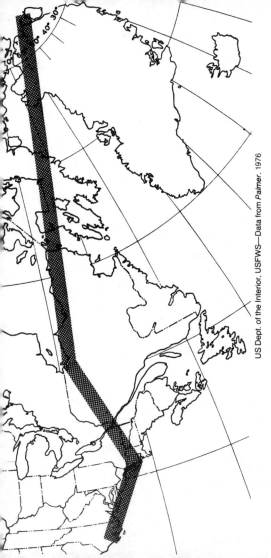

US Dept. of the Interior, USFWS—Data from *Palmer*, 1976

Fig. 8—Migration route of the Atlantic brant from breeding grounds along the northern Greenland Coast, Ellesmere Island and Baffin Island to wintering grounds along the Middle Atlantic Coast.

Matthew C. Perry, USFWS

from the Latin barnacle, a crustacean for some reason associated with the brant. *Hrota* is Icelandic for brant, and *nigrescens* refers to the darker plumage of the black brant.

The Atlantic brant is apparently the northernmost nesting bird in the world, slightly surpassing the greater snow goose for that honor. It nests mainly along the northern coast of Greenland, and on Baffin, Ellesmere, and Prince Patrick Islands (4).

Our eastern brant departs from the nesting grounds in late summer. One of the main routes south takes birds to James Bay, at the south end of Hudson Bay, a major

Fig. 9—During the severe winter of 1977 when bays, inlets and marshes were frozen, some brant fed on front lawns in residential areas bordering the Middle Atlantic Coast. Nearly one third of the Atlantic brant population perished during that winter.

Fig. 10—Brant (below) feeding on alga known as *Enteromorpha*, **a greenish material covering some of the oyster shells.**

Mike Haramis, USFWS

staging area for the push toward wintering grounds (Fig. 8). Brant arrive at James Bay by early October, and Long Island Sound, usually on the first stop after leaving James Bay, by mid-October, and arrive at Chincoteague by late October. A smaller contingent migrates across Labrador down the New England Coast, and a few cross the Atlantic to winter in Ireland.

In most years more brant winter in New Jersey than elsewhere along the Atlantic Coast. Barnegat Bay is one of the traditional wintering areas in that state. Chincoteague also is a regular wintering ground. Annual Christmas Counts at several coastal stations give good comparative population estimates for the winter range.

	1960	1974
Cape Cod, Massachusetts	2,500	1,131
S. Nassau County, L.I., New York	27,000	21,700
Barnegat, New Jersey	22,000	4,053
Oceanville, New Jersey	36,000	7,300
Cape May, New Jersey	40,000	10,400
Rehoboth Beach, Delaware	15,400	1,816
Ocean City, Maryland	6,000	1,045
Chincoteague, Virginia	8,000	6,118

Brant populations fluctuate considerably, often from one year to another. Such fluctuations may be due to predation or storms on the nesting grounds where nests and eggs and young are destroyed; reduction in food supply, such as the disappearance of eelgrass, a favorite food in the early 1930's, or the devastating effect on the popu-

Fig. 11—Atlantic brant over Chincoteague Bay (right). Brant usually fly low over the water, and seldom in formation like many other waterfowl.
And here (below) they are loafing in the frozen shallow water in January, 1978, at Chincoteague.

lation in extremely cold winters when it is impossible to obtain food from the frozen substrate in some sections.

Before the disappearance of eelgrass in 1931, that submerged aquatic plant formed 85 percent of the brant's diet. They fed on rootstocks and leaves. Leaves more than 30 inches in length have been found folded in stomachs. With the mysterious disappearance of eelgrass, by 1932 that plant formed only 8.5 percent of the brant's food.

Then there was a population decline for several years following. But the birds survived by adapting to other foods such as sea lettuce and other algae, widgeon grass, sedges, cordgrass, small mollusks, and some upland grazing.

In the winter of 1977, eighth coldest since the U.S. Weather Service began keeping records in the 1870s,

Mike Haramis, USFWS

thousands perished, especially in the more northern part of the winter range. In the New Jersey coastal area, 50,000 were estimated to have died. Because of the devastating 1977 winter, the following fall (November, 1977) population was down to about 55,000 birds. Prior to the 1977 winter freeze-up, the 1976 fall population was estimated at 115,000 birds. During the 1977 "deep freeze" many brant that survived did much of their feeding on front lawns of coastal residential areas (Fig. 9).

The winter of 1978 was somewhat of a repeat of that of 1977, but with January temperatures averaging four or five degrees warmer. Yet there were reports of some brant die-offs in New Jersey, although on a much smaller scale than in the previous winter.

On January 29, 1978, Mike Haramis and I counted about 500 healthy brant at Chincoteague in three hours of bird-watching. Virtually all tidal waters were open. We saw a few brant feeding on front lawns of homes, but most were in the salt marshes. Some that we got close to were feeding at the water's edge on an alga known as *Enteromorpha*, a greenish slimy material covering some ribbed mussels and oyster shells (Fig. 10).

Those foraging out in the shallow embayments were observed to "tip up" like puddle ducks in the course of food gathering. Most were in small groups of a half dozen or less, probably family groups, but several flocks of 50 or so (Fig. 11) were seen at several places. At other times in mid-winter I have seen rafts of two to three hundred in Chincoteague Bay.

The first spring departure from the Virginia coast is usually in late February, with the bulk of the birds moving up the coast in March. Some arrive at the Gulf of St. Lawrence in Canada by mid-April and James Bay or Ungava Bay in northern Quebec by the first part of May. They arrive on Arctic breeding grounds by mid-June. A few non-breeding birds apparently spend the summer in the Chincoteague area, just as a few northern ducks, Canada geese, and whistling swans also may be seen in Chesapeake Bay at that time. Some of these summer birds are thought to be cripples from the past fall and winter hunting season. Five that John Taylor and I saw in Assateague Bay off the north end of Chincoteague Island in early June, 1977, seemed healthy and were in flight when we saw them.

The Greater Snow Goose

Fig. 12—Snow geese (above). Greater snow geese (left) over Chincoteague, about the center of their winter range.

"From land beyond the north wind" (say the Eskimos), comes the greater snow goose (Figs. 12, 13) to the Virginia coast each winter. Its nesting ground is in the High Arctic, thus many years ago it was given the scientific name *Chen hyperborea atlanticus. Chen* is Greek for goose; *hyperborea,* also from the Greek, refers to the far north or beyond the north wind. *Atlanticus* refers to the winter range along the Middle Atlantic Coast. For technical reasons the scientific name has recently been changed so that it currently is *Anser caerulescens atlanticus.*

The greater snow goose's relative, a subspecies or variety known as the lesser snow goose, has two color phases, white and blue, and has a somewhat

Matthew C. Perry, USFWS

different geographic range. The greater snow goose population is a discrete one, with no blue phase birds.

Greater snow geese breed in the northeastern areas of the Arctic, mainly on Baffin and Ellesmere Islands and the northwest coast of Greenland. The lesser snow goose breeds in the Low Arctic (generally farther west of the greater's range) in Canada, Alaska and nearby Wrangle Island, USSR (4). Most lesser snows migrate along the Mississippi, Central (Great Plains), and Pacific Flyways, wintering chiefly along the Gulf Coast of Louisiana and Texas, in Mexico and California. In recent years about 3,000 lessers, including both white and blue phases, have been wintering at Blackwater National Wildlife Refuge near Cambridge, Maryland, in the Chesapeake Bay Country.

Greater snow geese leave the breeding grounds in late August and early September when the water and soil begin to freeze. They follow nearly the same route during spring and fall migration. About a month after leaving the Arctic breeding grounds, usually in early October, they have reached Cap Tourmente along the St. Lawrence River, where they rest and feed for eight or ten weeks before heading for the Middle Atlantic Coast.

13

At Cap Tourmente, which is located about 40 miles east of Quebec, they feed in the marshes, primarily on the rhizomes or roots of a sedge known as common three-square (*Scirpus americana*). From the St. Lawrence River, they fly virtually nonstop to Delaware Bay, from which most of them gradually shift southward along the coast to Chincoteague, Back Bay, and Mackay Island, Virginia, and to Pea Island, North Carolina (5). A few winter in the marshes of the Delaware River and Bay and the Atlantic coast of New Jersey. The first greater snows usually arrive at Chincoteague by the second half of October, and can usually be seen there on any day during the winter. Some 21,000 were seen on the one-day Christmas Count at Chincoteague, December, 1976.

The greater snow goose is more of a saltwater bird than the lesser snow. Its principal foods on the wintering grounds are the roots and culms of salt-marsh cordgrass (*Spartina alterniflora*) and bulrushes (*Scirpus robustus*). But from time to time it frequents brackish marshes to feed on Olney three-square (*Scirpus olneyi*), and freshwater areas where it forages on spike rush (*Eleocharis*), common three-square, and cattails (*Typha*). Their method of foraging sometimes has a devastating effect on a marsh; and as one refuge manager says, "they tear up the marsh like hogs." Sometimes, also, they feed in winter wheat fields located near the coast, and may be a problem for farmers.

Northward migration from the North Carolina and Virginia coasts begins about the third week in February, when birds assemble in large congregations and start moving northward toward Delaware Bay. This has been one of the regular staging areas for many years in both spring and fall. From Delaware Bay, greater snows proceed toward the High Arctic nesting grounds crossing over New England and stopping at Cap Tourmente on the St. Lawrence River, as they do in the fall migration. They depart from there in May, reaching the Arctic in the latter part of that month or in early June, as the northern breeding grounds begin to thaw.

I find it strange that upon visiting the Virginia coast in May and June, I always find a few brant, but rarely any snow geese, even though both nest in the same general area of the High Arctic. Perhaps some of the 500 brant that I saw in the Virginia coastal marshes on May 3, 1978, were non-breeding birds.

The total population of greater snow geese in the late fall of 1977 was estimated by the U.S. Fish and Wildlife Service to be 150,000 birds.

Fig. 13—Snow geese resting in salt meadow on Assateague Island in January. Note dusky-colored immatures in center of picture.

C. Edward Addy, observing waterfowl along the Delmarva Coast at Bethany Beach, Delaware, on October 17, 1970, noted a massive southward migration of scoters. Flocks passing by during the day probably totaled over a million birds. Ed Addy at that time was a waterfowl biologist with the U.S. Fish and Wildlife Service, and was well trained in estimating numbers of ducks.

Fig. 14—Three species of scoters—white-winged, surf, and black—occur along the Virginia coast in winter. These sea ducks often fly in single file close to the water.

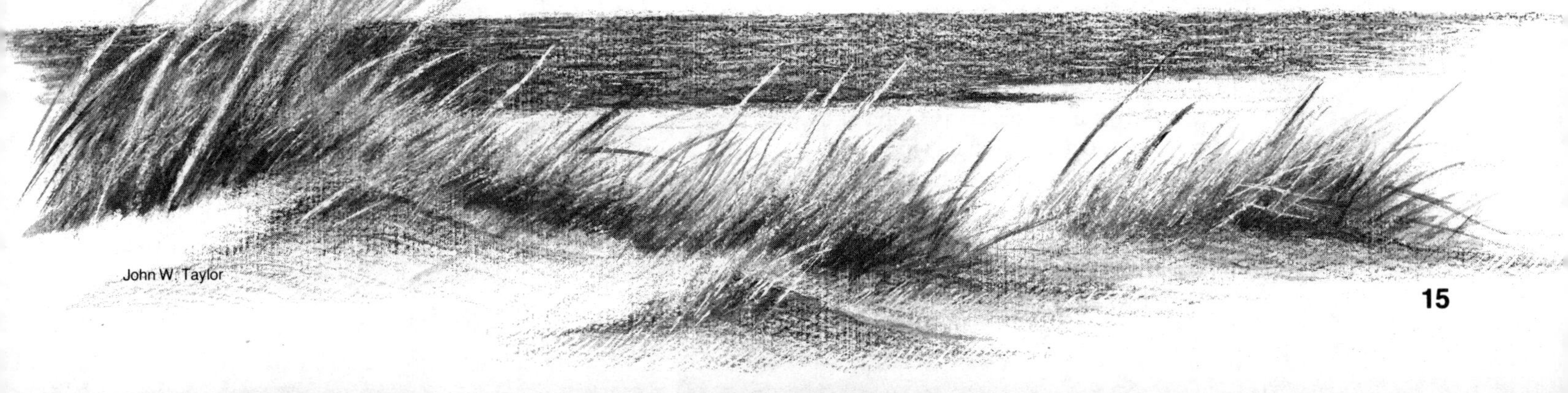

John W. Taylor

15

Since most scoters wintering in the east occur at that season along the New England and Middle Atlantic Coasts and embayments, most of those passing Bethany Beach, which is about six miles north of the Maryland line, were probably destined for offshore waters along southern Delmarva and the lower Chesapeake Bay.

Sea coots, as scoters are known to some of the local hunters because of their resemblance to the American coot, a bird of inland waters, are regularly recorded each winter on the Chincoteague and Cape Charles Christmas Counts. In Virginia coastal waters, the surf and the common or black scoters apparently are more abundant than the white-winged scoter.

Scoters are large chunky black sea ducks. Males are blackish while females are blackish-brown or sooty in color. The male white-winged scoter is the heaviest, weighing up to four pounds, and is the easiest to identify because of its white speculum or wing patch. The characteristic flight of scoters is a long undulating line just over the tops of the ocean waves (Fig. 14).

Other wintering coastal sea ducks are the oldsquaw, scaup, eiders, and the harlequin duck. The oldsquaw or "South-southerly," a name by which it is better known in some quarters, is a common winter resident along the Virginia coast; but the two species of eiders, king and common, and the harlequin duck are rather rare this far south.

The oldsquaw (Fig. 15) is a trim little sea duck that because of its long tail looks a little like a pintail, except that it is smaller and does not have the long neck of the latter. Clarence Cottam, one of my former mentors, characterizes this species so well in his publication, *Food Habits of North American Diving Ducks* (6):

Because it is so lively, showy, and clamorous, the old squaw [sic] is familiar to every fisherman, shore shooter, and naturalist who frequents the waters of any northern coast. It is known by more than a score of local names, most of which are descriptive of appearance or habit. Among them may be noted longtail, pintail or sea pintail, fish duck, cockertail, swallowtail, noisy duck, South-southerly, coween, old-granny, and old wife. The last two names as well as the term "old sqaw," were probably given because the bird is so loquacious. Drifting ice floes, noisy seas, and arctic winds seem to form a congenial habitat for this hardy and handsome duck. Attractive dress and posture, characteristic social posture, and instinctive and almost incessant yet pleasing babble give it a truly striking personality that immeasurably enlivens an otherwise dreary coast.

Oldsquaws nest farther north in larger numbers than any other ducks, and are circumpolar in breeding distribution. They nest along the Greenland and Iceland Coasts and in the Canadian Arctic tundra north of the Arctic Circle.

One-day Christmas Counts of oldsquaws at Chincoteague and Cape Charles in 1975 were 2,485 and 1,046 respectively.

Oldsquaws, scoters, scaup and other diving ducks along the coast feed largely on crustaceans, including mud crabs, blue crabs, shrimps, crayfish, and sandbugs (also a crustacean), mollusks, fish, insects, and submerged aquatic plants.

The oldsquaw is known to dive deeper than most other waterfowl. They have been taken in gill nets at depths of 150 feet, although they normally feed in much shallower depths, more like 25 or 30 feet.

Two other ducks regularly occurring just offshore in the ocean are the common goldeneye and black duck. Since most of the ducks that occur in the oceanic littoral zone are divers, the presence of the goldeneye would not be unexpected. However, the black duck is a dabbler or puddle duck that feeds on or close to the surface, and is usually identified with shoal-water habitats. It does occur more frequently in the embayments behind the barrier islands where it is the most abundant and most often hunted wild duck.

Two species of loons, the common (Fig. 16) and red-throated are found regularly in the ocean off the Middle Atlantic Coast and in the coastal embayments. On the 1970 (December 28) Christmas Count at Chincoteague, 641 common and 108 red-throated loons were reported. On March 10, 1971, C.R. Vaughn reported 5,000 red-throated loons off Wallops Island, Virginia: "The birds were in small groups (up to 20) and extended the entire eight-mile length of the island and up to one mile off-shore." (7).

As for identification, the smaller red-throated loon can be differentiated from the common by its slightly up-tilted bill.

Bob Hines, USFWS

Fig. 15—The oldsquaw, one of the few local Arctic breeding ducks, regularly winters as far south along the Atlantic Coast as Virginia. It occurs in the coastal embayments, oceanic littoral zone, and well out in the ocean—sometimes miles from land.

Fig. 16—The common loon is numerous during the winter half of the year in the oceanic littoral zone and the coastal embayments. It spends the summer on northern wilderness lakes.

The common loon is known for its variety of wild and eerie calls, most often heard from the lonely Northwoods' wilderness lakes where it nests. Ralph Palmer, editor of the *Handbook of North American Birds* (8) and other authors characterize these different calls as "tremolo," "yodel," "wail," and "talking," each given under different circumstances and mostly related to courtship, mating, and dual feeding activities. The tremolo call has been referred to as "loon laughter." On two occasions while deep in the heart of the Great Dismal Swamp in early spring, I heard the tremolo calling of a migrating common loon directly overhead and just over the treetops, and I must say that it startled me more than any other strange sound that I ever heard in that swamp.

Probably no bird is more closely associated with the oceanic littoral zone than the double-crested cormorant. This large black bird that may be seen at any season of the year perched upright on pilings (Fig. 17), is especially numerous during migrations along the oceanfront and above the coastal embayments. Cormorants usually fly just above the surface of the water in a single line. But when migrating they sometimes fly higher and in a ragged "V" formation. During the first week in May, 1978, I observed northward flights of several thousand cormorants over Chincoteague Bay and along the oceanfront at Assateague Island. Banding records seem to indicate that these migrants were headed for breeding grounds in Maine, Ontario, or Quebec.

Fig. 17—Known by its blackish plumage and its upright posture when it perches (right), the cormorant can also be seen flying with outstretched neck in single file close to water. (below right) Cormorants on a fish trap.

Bob Hines, USFWS

From the bird-watchers' point of view, probably the most eagerly sought birds of the oceanic littoral zone are the pelagic species, those of the high seas that occasionally occur near shore by accident rather than design. Such are the shearwaters, gannets, kittiwakes, skuas, fulmars, petrels, razorbills, dovekies, murres, guillemots, and several of the phalaropes. Most of these oceanic species that come from the Arctic or Antarctic appear in the latitude of the Eastern Shore of Virginia during the winter half of the year. They seldom come closer than ten or fifteen miles from shore, and most regularly occur at the edge of the Continental Shelf, 50-60 miles east of land in the main commercial fishing lanes and the Gulf Stream.

Pelagic birds also follow whales and other sea mammals for the same reason that they follow ships, for the scraps of food left behind in the wake. When a whale surfaces and blows, particles of food are discharged along with the spouting water.

Fred Scott (9), editor of the *Raven*, reported that on September 7, 1974, at the mouth of Chesapeake Bay, R.L.

Ake observed a black-legged kittiwake feeding by dabbling in the water over a pod of porpoises; and on July 3, 1975, M.A. Byrd, Rae Lea, and Jack Stevens were in Mobjack Bay, on the west side of the Chesapeake Bay where they watched a school of porpoises diving within 20 yards of their boat. The bay was smooth, and virtually no birds were in sight. In a few minutes, 45 Wilson's petrels had assembled and begun to feed on the surface of the waters where the porpoises were diving. As the observers followed the marine mammals, it was clear that the petrels were following too, evidently for purposes of obtaining food items brought to the surface by the animals.

Robert B. McCartney, an ornithologist in the USFWS and stationed on a lightship about 20 miles off Chinco-

teague, observed a number of pelagic species during his tour of duty, including several hundred Cory's shearwaters in a single day, between June and October, 1954; a great skua on January 1, 1955; and as many as 15 black-legged kittiwakes daily between late November, 1954, and March, 1955, (10).

In some years there are great incursions of Arctic pelagics in our offshore waters. The dovekie, smallest member of the family Alcidae (auks, murres, puffins, etc.) inhabiting Atlantic coastal waters, migrated in great numbers southward beyond its normal winter range during several winters in the 1930s and 1940s. Many died and were washed up along the coastal beaches. During early January, 1949, John Buckalew reported that thousands occurred at 10-15 miles off of Ocean City, Maryland, with hundreds caught in mackerel nets; and on February 5, 1940, R.H. Pough, on a steamboat off the coast of Virginia, states that dovekies were flushed at the rate of 25-50 per hour (11).

Many of the earliest records of species of pelagic birds on the Virginia bird list were based on specimens that had died at sea, washed ashore and eventually were picked up along a beach. Many such specimens from Virginia beaches were deposited in museum collections, and include the sooty, Audubon's, and greater shearwaters, razorbill, thick-billed murre, dovekie, and long-tailed jaeger.

There have been numerous observations of pelagics: earlier, from the Cape Charles-Little Creek Ferry, and, recently, from the bridge-tunnel that has replaced it. Species frequently seen there are gannets, Wilson's petrels, and parasitic jaegers. This also is one of the best places to see a variety of gulls and terns, the former especially in winter and the latter in summer. At least nine species of gulls have been recorded from the general area, and include such rarities as the glaucous, Iceland, black-headed, and little gulls, as well as the more common species, herring, ring-billed, great black-backed, Bonapart's, and laughing. The laughing gull is the most common breeding form of the Virginia coast, and is a summer resident, although one or two are occasionally reported on one of the local Christmas Counts. There have also been eleven species of terns reported from the Virginia coast. Seven presently nest there: the common, little or least, gull-billed, royal, Sandwich, Forster's, and Caspian. The Caspian is a very rare nesting bird in the area, but occurs regularly during migration. The roseate apparently has nested there in the past, and the black tern is a migrant.

The loons, the sea ducks, the pelagic or oceanic species from the Arctic and Antarctic, the frigatebirds from the tropics, the rare gulls, the variety of terns, and the sandpipers and plovers winging their way along the surf line are all a part of the avifauna that lures the bird-watcher to the oceanic littoral zone.

Breeding Birds of the Salt Marshes

The salt marsh is perhaps the least disturbed of the natural areas of the Coastal Plain, and in a sense is the last frontier in Eastern North America. Several million acres stretch from New England to Florida, chiefly behind the coastal barrier islands (Fig. 18).

The predominant vegetation of coastal salt marshes is salt-marsh cordgrass (*Spartina alterniflora*). This plant grows in uniform stands, but at different heights in different zones. Along some sections of the coast it varies in height from ten inches to six feet. This is due mainly to

Fig. 18—Laughing gull at nest in salt marsh near Chincoteague, May, 1978. In recent years several hundred pairs have nested in the marshes on both sides of the causeway leading into town.

Fig. 19—Nest and eggs of gadwall on marshy island in Assateague Bay near Chincoteague, Virginia, June 4, 1977.

cordgrass sensitivity to water level. The taller cordgrass grows along the edge of tidal guts. The shortgrass zone is farther from the gut and intergrades with the salt meadow. Extensive stands of needlerush (*Juncus roemarianus*) border sections of the salt-marsh cordgrass, usually on the back or landward side of marshes. This is a rather sterile marsh type for wildlife compared to salt-marsh cordgrass or salt meadow.

In the higher and drier parts of most salt marshes, the salt meadow is the predominant plant community. Salt-meadow cordgrass (*Spartina patens*) and salt-grass (*Distichlis spicata*) are the principal species. Both of these grasses grow only about a foot or so in height, and are usually windblown, thus giving this kind of marsh a meadowlike appearance. The salt meadow is usually covered with water only by spring or flood tides, while much of the salt-marsh cordgrass zone is flooded twice daily.

The salt marshes are the nesting and feeding grounds of a wide variety of birds. Some are colonial nesting birds like the laughing gull and Forster's tern; others, like the clapper rail, willet, black duck and seaside and sharp-tailed sparrows are abundant, but their nests are strung out through the marsh rather than in colonies.

There are large expanses of marsh, many acres, in which there are very few nesting birds, while on the other

Fig. 20—Nest and eggs of Forster's tern built on wrack
(an accumulation of dead aquatic plants) in salt
marsh at Wire Narrows, near Chincoteague, May 26, 1978.
Other native tern species nest on the barrier beaches.

Fig. 21—Nest and eggs of Forster's tern on small marshy island in Assateague
Bay, near Chincoteague, Virginia, June 3, 1977. Blackish object to left of nest is a
meadow vole (mouse). Note tern egg to right of nest, and shell and claw of blue crab.
The vole, egg, and crab may have been objects of food left by laughing or
herring gulls that fed in this Forster's tern nesting colony,
or were deposited in this low area of the salt marsh by a flood tide.

hand, a small quarter of an acre island in an embayment may be packed with colonial nesters. One such island in Assateague Bay, lying between the north end of Chincoteague Island and the barrier beach, Assateague, that John Taylor and I examined on June 3, 1977, had the following nesting birds: 38 active nests of two or three eggs each of the Forster's tern, a gadwall's nest of ten eggs (Fig. 19), and one nest each of a clapper rail, willet, American oystercatcher, seaside sparrow, and song sparrow.

The Forster's tern, unlike the other six or seven species of terns that nest along the ocean beaches of the Virginia Barrier Islands, is a marsh nesting bird. Their nesting habits are similar to those of the laughing gull, and occasionally Forster's tern nests are located in these gull colonies.

On the small island in Assateague Bay, most of the tern nests were located in the wrack area—an accumulation of dead marsh grasses and submergent aquatic vegetation such as eelgrass, that has been carried by an abnormally high tide into the marsh. As the tide recedes, the accumulation of flotsam or dead vegetation lodges in the taller growth of standing salt-marsh cordgrass that grows beside a tidal gut. Thus the wrack is a long line of packed debris that is extended in a single line following the contour of the edge or margin of the marsh, sometimes with the shape of a small serpentine wall. Nests are located on top of the wrack, which is often about a foot in height, and above normal high tide (Fig. 20). Many laughing gull nests are placed in the wrack. A few Forster's tern nests on the small marshy island were located in bare spots that were formerly pools of water that had dried-up (Fig. 21). Such spots were near the center of the island and nests were built-up to about a foot in height, compared to those on the wrack, which were only three or four inches in height on the one-foot high wrack. Strewn about these bare spots were pieces of blue crabs and other food items, including a dead field mouse (*Microtus*). The crabs and the mouse may have been brought to these low bare spots to be fed upon by herring, great black-backed, or laughing gulls; or were deposited there by a flood tide.

The black duck is the characteristic breeding waterfowl species of the salt marsh. Gadwall's and blue-winged teal, while present, are not as common in this area, but gadwalls seem to be increasing.

Black ducks not only nest in the predominantly salt-marsh cordgrass, but also in the higher and more restricted salt meadow, and in a number of other sites, including the top of duck blinds that are covered with brush or cedar branches; rarely they nest in an old hawk's or crow's nest high in a loblolly pine.

One of the best places to see salt-marsh birds along the Virginia Coastal Strand is from the Chincoteague Causeway. Go in winter for brant, snow geese, and other waterfowl; late spring and summer for shorebirds, large waders, boat-tailed grackles, and clapper rails; and May, June, and early July for nesting laughing gulls.

Fig. 22—The marsh hen, or clapper rail,
is the typical bird of the coastal salt marsh. Most
of them nest in the taller stands of salt-marsh
cordgrass that grows along the edge
of the tidal guts. Clutch size is usually 10-11 eggs.

The Marsh Hen

The clapper rail, as the marsh hen is also called, is more closely identified with the coastal marsh than any other bird. Salt marsh hunters know it, ornithologists birding in coastal areas seek it out, and watermen who live at

25

Chincoteague and other ports along the Virginia Coastal Strand know it by its loud discordant calls, which they associate with the changing tides. It is a bird of the salt-marsh cordgrass, spending virtually all of its time in this marsh community, wandering to its edge to feed on the mud flats at low tide.

The rails are probably the most "grounded" family of birds. Extended flights by North American species are made mainly when migrating. On the breeding grounds they occasionally fly across a tidal gut or take off for a short distance when suddenly flushed. Since they spend most of their time walking or running, they are often referred to as weak fliers. In fact, in some remote parts of the world species of rails that live on islands where there have been no predators are flightless. However, the marsh hen or clapper rail actually is a strong flyer that when flushed flies only a short distance because it wants to descend to cover in a hurry.

The call of the marsh hen may be heard at any time during the 24-hour period. The primary advertising call, the one most often heard throughout the year, has been variously described as *cac-cac-cac-* or *chac-chac-chac-* or *jupe-jupe-jupe-*. As one bird begins to sound off there is a chain reaction and others join in.

With the onset of the breeding season, in April and May, rails become noisier, and a new sound, along with the primary advertising call is heard on the marsh—the mating call of the male marsh hen. The *kik-kik-kik-* mating call of the marsh hen or clapper rail and the king

rail of fresher marshes, sound identical, and sometimes may be heard continuously from one individual male for ten minutes.

The mating call is given on the male's breeding or nesting territory, a parcel of land staked out and defended from other marsh hens during the breeding season. After the pair bond is formed, the male and female also have a variety of other calls, mostly subdued, to keep in touch with each other when they wander apart while feeding.

Most marsh hens build their nests (Fig. 22) along the edge of the narrow tidal guts that thread their way through the marsh. The cordgrass is taller in this zone where the tide is highest and more sediment accumulates and builds a small levee along the bank of the gut. Just behind this tall cordgrass strip is the wrack, an accumulation of flotsam upon which laughing gulls and Forster's terns often build their nests. Often the exposed nest of a gull or tern is only five or six feet from a well-hidden marsh hen's nest. A marsh hen will tolerate nests of other species at such close range, but not that of another of its kind. J.J. Murray (12) found a marsh hen nest at Cobb's Island directly between two Forster's tern nests that were four and a half feet apart.

The marsh hen's nest is placed but a few inches above the mean high-tide level, and has a canopy which conceals the eggs pretty well from predators, as well as a ramp for easy access and a quick exodus.

The nesting density in some sections of marsh is high, and in 1950, in a 47-acre tract of salt-marsh cordgrass,

Robert E. Stewart found 79 occupied nests. Eighty percent of the nests were located in the tall growth of salt-marsh cordgrass within 15 feet of a tidal gut or creek.

Marsh hens lay large clutches of eggs (Fig. 23). This compensates for the loss of so many clutches when spring or flood tides occur during the nesting season, and inundate the marsh (Fig. 24). The clutch size during first nesting attempts averages nine or ten eggs. Nesting activity peaks in the latter half of May and first week of June. Renesting attempts following destruction of initial clutches by high tides or predation may continue well into July. M.A. Byrd, Gary Seek, and Bill Smith (13) located 16 clapper rail nests on Gull Marsh near Cobb's Island on July 23, 1971. This would be later than average for second clutches or renestings. Young produced from these late nestings would not reach flight age until at least mid-September. Clutches of renesting or second attempts at Chincoteague averaged only five eggs (14).

Raccoons and fish crows are the principal predators of marsh hen nests. But most nests are so well hidden and the birds are so secretive that they are seldom located by fish crows hovering over the marshes in search of eggs. In New Jersey one rail or marsh hen clutch was successfully hatched in a nest located less than 25 feet from a power pole on which a pair of fish crows had an active nest (15).

But storm tides can wreak havoc in a rail nesting marsh. O.S. Pettingill, Jr., (16) was witness to one such tide on Cobb's Island:

> During the high tide I stayed in Captain George W. Cobb's house. This was ideally located on the southern end of the island and afforded an extensive view of a large portion of the island to the north. Placed back from the beach behind a ridge of sand dunes, the house rested on piles some seven or eight feet above the salt marsh that began below the house and stretched far northwestward and westward. Protected from high water and the surf, it was a safe place under such conditions.
>
> The tide that occurred on this day completely inundated the marsh and came to within one foot of the floor of Captain Cobb's house. While this tide was rising, I counted six pairs of adult Clapper Rails and their broods swimming above the marsh, striving desperately to reach the dunes, which were the only parts of the island still above water. The northeast wind was driving them to the southward and made their attempts at reaching shore seemingly useless. Two broods ultimately came ashore; three others were swept past the southern point of the island to death in the rough ocean. The sixth brood was blown directly toward the house. My attention

was naturally directed toward the welfare of the family group.

As this brood rapidly drifted toward the house I was able to discern seven young birds, all of which were about of an equal age. I judged that they were two weeks old. They were barely able to keep their heads and backs above water. Waves, freshly whipped up by the wind, continually washed over them, soaking their down and making them less buoyant each time. They seemed about to succumb and were making no attempts to swim. The two parent birds, however, were large enough and strong enough to keep their heads above the waves breaking over them and were swimming anxiously about their young. Every now and then the old birds would head toward the dunes, but seeing that their offspring were not following, would turn back and continue encircling them. In a very short time the rail family was floating along past the house.

Captain Cobb and I soon rescued the seven young birds by plunging into the water and gathering them up and bringing them to the porch. We placed them in a carton two feet square and closed the four flaps. As a result of our interference the parent birds made away to the sand dunes calling loudly. Darkness set in before the tide went out, and the young rails passed the night in the carton on the porch. While their down was soaked and they seemed utterly exhaust-

Fig. 23—Nest and eggs of clapper rail in salt-marsh cordgrass at Chincoteague, June, 1977.

ed, scarcely moving when we touched them, they were old enough and the temperature of the surrounding air was warm enough to permit their survival without brooding.

According to Pettingill, the next day the young were coaxed out of the box by the parents and all hurried off into the marsh.

Fig. 24—Dead marsh grass left on wharf as flood tide receded along Gargathy Creek near Metomkin Island. Clapper rails are common nesting birds in the salt marsh across the creek. If the flood tide had occurred a month later at the height of the nesting season in late May, 1978, virtually all nests would have been destroyed.

Fig. 25—A day-old clapper rail chick is as black as a piece of coal.

It takes a young marsh hen (Fig. 25) about two months to reach flying stage, which along the coast of Virginia is seldom before early August. During midsummer, many adults are undergoing a postnuptial molt, which involves a simultaneous losing of the flight feathers, leaving them flightless for about a month. Robert E. Stewart (17) trapped and banded many clapper rails or marsh hens at Chincoteague, and made the following notes regarding their molt:

During the trapping period (July 16-August 31) most of the adults were undergoing their postnuptial molt...The individual molting period lasts about one month. The first adult observed in full molt was trapped on July 21. During the period August 24 to August 31 (the period just before hunting season) a total of 11 adults were trapped. Of these only five had completed their molt and were capable of flight, while four were in heavy molt, and were completely flightless. Surprisingly enough the other two adults had not even started to molt and were in very worn plumage.

September marks the opening of the marsh hen hunting season. Hunting is done mostly when there is a "Marsh Hen Tide." Such a tide occurs when a north wind pushes the normal high tide up even higher. Under these conditions a boat can be poled through the marsh grass, flushing the birds.

September is also the time when many Chincoteague marsh hens begin their departure for the wintering grounds located along South Atlantic coastal marshes from North Carolina to northern Florida.

According to R.E. Stewart (18) who, with an assist from John H. Buckalew and Gorman Bond, banded over a thousand marsh hens at Chincoteague in 1950 and 1951, some of these rails waste little time in traveling from their breeding grounds to the wintering area. This is indicated by an immature bird that was banded at Chincoteague on August 26, 1950, and recovered in northeastern Florida on September 24, 1950. Other evidence that some of the rails migrate early is furnished by the record of one banded at Chincoteague on August 15, 1950, and recovered about 60 miles to the south on September 6, 1950. Another banded at Chincoteague on July 28, 1951, was recovered in South Carolina on September 16, 1951.

An interesting note has been contributed by Adams and Quay (19) regarding hazards sometimes encountered by migrating marsh hens:

At dusk on September 20, 1955, 'hundreds' of clapper rails invaded Carolina Beach, N.C., preceding and during a heavy fog. The birds became confused and entered shops, flew into cars and people, perched on telephone wires and houses, etc. (*John H. Farrell*, pers. comm.).

E.O. Mellinger

Fig. 26—Fiddler crabs on mud flat (far left) at edge of salt marsh. Fiddlers are an important food of clapper rails, willets, boat-tailed grackles, whimbrels (Hudsonian curlews), and several other species of birds of the Virginia Coastal Strand.

Fig. 27—Periwinkle snails climbing up stems of salt-marsh cordgrass (left) as the tide slowly rises in the marsh. They are ingested whole by the rail, and John Oney reports that 48 have been found in a single stomach.

Wintering marsh hen populations at Chincoteague and other coastal marsh areas along the coast of Virginia apparently are higher than one might surmise. While the one-day Christmas Counts at Chincoteague in late December seldom report more than 25 birds, those at Cape Charles have been as high as 146 on December 27, 1964, and 155 on December 27, 1971. Higher counts at Cape Charles may be due to a "ganging up" of birds as they are confronted by the wide mouth of Chesapeake Bay; and also, there are usually more participants at Cape Charles than Chincoteague.

Foods and Feeding Behavior. The principal foods of marsh hens in most Middle Atlantic coastal marshes are fiddler crabs (Fig. 26). Secondary foods are several forms of snails, including the periwinkle (Fig. 27) aquatic insects, and small clams.

The snails and clams usually are swallowed whole, but the fiddler crabs, unless extremely small, are usually dismantled before ingestion. The marsh hen usually grabs the male fiddler by its larger claw, shakes it vigorously until the body is disengaged, and then retrieves the scrambling fiddler a few feet away and swallows it. During the courtship and mating period the male often will catch a fiddler crab and run to its mate to present it to her while she is foraging for herself.

John W. Taylor

Fig. 28—Laughing gulls in summer or breeding plumage. This is the original native gull of the Virginia coast.

The Laughing Gull

The most striking feature of the summer birdlife of the Virginia Coastal Strand is the laughing gull (Fig. 28). It is gone in winter to warmer climes, and its place of prominence at that season is taken by herring and ring-billed gulls and several kinds of waterfowl. But during the summer half of the year laughing gulls are everywhere—flying over Chincoteague and other coastal villages, nesting in the salt marshes, hunting for soft crabs along the edge of a shallow embayment, or coursing back and forth above the surf line. They are known at once by their black heads and the dark carmine of their bills and feet. The name comes from the high pitched laughing call notes, *ha-ha-ha-haah-haah-haah-*. The local people refer to them as black-headed gulls. This is the familiar name along the Virginia Coastal Strand, but not for broader use, as there are several species of gulls with black heads.

As they work their way northward in the spring their advance coincides with the season of spring plowing along the Coastal Plain, and they flock to the newly turned earth and its largesse of earthworms and grubs. They arrive along the Virginia coast in late March. By the first of May, laughing gulls have pretty well settled down on their nesting grounds and courtship is under way. They are colonial nesting birds whose colonies sometimes number several thousand pairs, and are usually located in the cordgrass marshes. Nests are placed near the tidal guts (Fig. 29).

Fig. 29—Nest and eggs of laughing gull (right) beside tidal gut (at low tide). Chincoteague, June 3, 1977. Nests are placed in wrack that accumulates at edge of salt marsh. Wrack is a good foundation or substrate for a nest, usually above normal high tide level, and is composed mainly of dead stems of cordgrass and eelgrass (above). Day-old laughing gull chick (above right) and pipped egg in nest in salt marsh near Chincoteague, June 15, 1978. This nest of a laughing gull (bottom right), near Chincoteague in May, 1978, was built on an old clapper rail banding trap used by Robert E. Stewart in 1950.

Clapper rails nest in the same spartina zone bordering tidal guts, but their nests are concealed by the tall salt-marsh cordgrass, while the laughing gull nests are completely exposed. Perhaps it is not as important for the gull to conceal its eggs since it is a large aggressive bird, and a good match in size and strength for one of its chief nest predators, the fish crow, that scouts the marshes for eggs.

A clapper rail's nest is sometimes located only three or four feet from a gull's, but there seems never to be any territorial dispute, as clutches hatch side by side. A.B. Howell found a clapper rail's nest and eggs at Cobb's

Fig. 30—Young laughing gull hiding in salt marsh. As we approached this young bird it regurgitated parts of a soft crab, one of several forms of crustaceans fed to fledgling laughing gulls. Chincoteague, July 7, 1977.

Island. It contained a laughing gull's egg (20). Also at Cobb's Island, J.J. Murray found a Forster's tern nest with two laughing gull eggs and one of the tern (12).

Laughing gull eggs are laid in late May. When I visited a colony of several hundred pairs at Chincoteague in the last week in May, 1978, most nests contained two or three eggs. By the middle of June, the first eggs were beginning to hatch. Three of sixty nests examined each had one newly-hatched chick.

One of the foods fed to the young (Fig. 30) that were about three-fourths grown were soft crabs (*Callinectes sapidus*). As I approached several of these young birds they regurgitated pieces of these crustaceans. John Buckalew, who has banded thousands of young laughing gulls, says that insects obtained by parent birds in nearby upland agricultural fields are also an important food of the young.

Adult laughing gulls and young that fend for themselves feed on a wide variety of foods; they select live food more often than does the herring gull, which is more of a scavenger. However, we have often seen laughing gulls following fishing vessels that were "chumming" to attract fish, or were throwing offal or fish scraps overboard (Fig. 31).

When nesting tern and laughing gull colonies are located close together, gulls sometimes commit depredations on eggs and newly-hatched chicks if some section of the tern colony is left unprotected.

Fig. 31—Laughing gulls following a fishing boat that is chumming (baiting for fish) or disposing of offal. Most gulls are scavengers, but also feed on crabs and other crustaceans, marine worms and mollusks. During the spring, flocks can be observed in plowed fields feeding on earthworms and grubs (insect larvae), and in summer they visit soybean and other crop fields to obtain various insects.

According to Sprunt and Chamberlain (21), along the South Carolina coast the laughing gull is at times piratical. It will rob a brown pelican of its prey by watching it dive, alighting on the pelican's head as it comes to the surface and snatching the fish.

Laughing gulls are among the latest native seabirds of the Virginia coast to migrate south in the fall. There are often a number of them about well into November; but by the end of that month, most have passed southward. Some winter along the South Atlantic Coast; others go all the way to the Caribbean Islands and the coasts of Central and northern South America. Vernon Kleen has had two interesting recoveries of wintering laughing gulls from South America. He banded the birds on islands in Chincoteague Bay (22). One banded on June 29, 1963, was recovered near Buenaventura, Colombia, February 20, 1964. Another, banded on June 30, 1963, was recovered near Tumaco, Colombia, January 29, 1964.

In winter the adult laughing gull looks much like the other large gulls, having molted its black head feathers. In some years one or two are reported on the Christmas Counts at Chincoteague or Cape Charles.

Strikers and Floodgulls

Fig. 32—The long, pointed wings of the tern (left) are characteristic of great flyers, birds that spend a lot of time in the air. Black skimmers (right) flying above the surfline.

"Strikers" and **"Floodgulls"** are colonial nesting birds of the seabeaches. "Striker" is a local name for the several species of native terns, the royal, common, little (formerly least), gull-billed, Forster's and Sandwich. The name "Striker" may have come from the tern's habit of striking the water with great velocity when diving for fish. "Sea Swallow" is another local name applied to the tern. Its beautiful streamlined body with forked tail, and manner of flying suggests the twisting, rolling flight of a barn swallow coursing the meadow. The tern's long pointed wings are typical of birds that spend much of their time flying (Figs. 32, 33).

"Floodgull" is a local name for the black skimmer (Fig. 34), whose time of feeding is influenced by the tide. A.C. Bent's explanation of this name as presented in his book, *Life Histories of North American Gulls and Terns*, (23) is interesting:

When the rising tide flows in around the island, covering the outer sand bars, driving the birds from their low-tide roosting and feeding places and flooding the shallow estuaries, then the 'flood gulls,' as they are called, may be seen skimming over the muddy shallows, about the mouths of the creeks, or up into the narrow inlets, gracefully gliding on their long, slender wings close to the surface in search of their finny prey, the tiny minnows, which have followed the advancing tide into the protecting shallows.

While the above explanation of their feeding behavior is a reason for the local name "Floodgull," black skimmers also feed at low tide.

Black skimmers and common terns nest separately, or together in the same colonies (Figs. 35, 36). R.M. Erwin (24), who made an intensive study of nesting colonies of skimmers and terns, says that the nesting of skimmers with common terns suggests that this relationship with an aggressive species (the tern) is to their advantage in avoiding egg predation by laughing and herring gulls.

Luther C. Goldman, USFWS

Fig. 33—Least or little terns (left) are fairly common summer residents of the Virginia Coastal Strand. They nest on the barrier beaches and sandy islands of some of the embayments. They are readily distinguished from the other species of terns by their small size, white forehead, and yellow bill (in spring and summer). Nest and eggs of least or little tern (above).

37

Fig. 34—Black skimmers (left)
heading for feeding grounds as the tide changes.

Fig. 35—Nesting colony (bottom left) of
black skimmers and common terns. Skimmers
almost always nest with common terns.

Fig. 36—Common tern at nest (right).
Along the Virginia coast these terns usually
nest in or near colonies of black
skimmers, least or little terns and royal terns.

Fig. 37—Nest and eggs of black skimmer (bottom)
at lower end of Assateague Island,
June, 1938. Nest in the sand is a mere
depression known as a "scrape."

Fig. 38—Nest and eggs of common tern (bottom right)
on barrier island beach, June 14, 1978.

Ralph Palmer

Some tern and skimmer nesting colonies are large (Fig. 42). In June, 1976, there were approximately 3,000 pairs of royal terns and 1,000 pairs of black skimmers nesting on Fisherman's Island near Cape Charles and the north end of the Chesapeake Bay Bridge-Tunnel. At Metomkin Island on June 19, 1976, Mitchell Byrd and associates (25) reported 1,665 pairs of black skimmers and 500 pairs of gull-billed terns. There were an estimated 2,000 pairs of least or little terns with eggs or young on Metomkin Island in June, 1978.

It is interesting to compare the size of some present-day colonies with those that existed at Cobb's Island in the latter part of the last century when terns were slaughtered for the millinery trade, and there were more people living on some of the Lower Eastern Shore barrier islands, most of which are presently uninhabited by man (*See* Table I).

Terns and skimmers nest on the barrier islands and on smaller spoil bank and natural islands in the embayments. The larger colonies are generally located on uninhabited barrier islands. Such colonies are often located near inlets, which are good food-gathering areas. The nest sites are usually located at a place on the beach where flood tides have deposited large quantities of shells, pebbles, and flotsam that help camouflage the speckled eggs (Figs. 39, 41). In some colonies, nests are placed so close together that it is almost impossible for a human being to walk through a colony without stepping on the eggs.

Samuel A. Grimes

Fig. 39—Least tern at nest (far left). There was a nesting colony of several hundred pairs on Metomkin Island in June, 1978. Least terns occur along the Virginia coast from late April to early September.

Such packed colonies probably minimize egg predation by predatory gulls.

The size of a nesting territory defended by a tern therefore may be only four or five inches surrounding the nest. This is quite a contrast to the size of the nesting territory of a small bird like a warbler or vireo that may defend one-half an acre, or that of a bald eagle that defends a territory of a square mile or larger.

A storm tide that floods a nesting colony, washing away eggs and young, will not discourage the birds from renesting. Following the flooding out of a colony, the birds are often forced to shift to a nearby site for a second try.

Terns and skimmers usually arrive on the breeding ground in mid- or late April, but nesting is seldom under way before late May. Nests on the beach are a mere depression in the sand (Fig. 37) known as a "scrape," and are made by a bird sitting down and revolving or turning around a few times. The common tern generally uses a little grass or straw to line its "scrape" or nest (Fig. 38).

As a part of the courtship ritual of terns and skimmers, before and during the period of egg laying, the male will return to the nesting colony from time to time carrying a fish, which, after strutting around a bit in front of the female, he will present to her. If the female is on the nest she will usually leave to accept the fish, and then will often allow the male to copulate with her. On several occasions I have seen a male use a piece of straw or a small piece of wood to accomplish the same purpose.

Most species of terns usually lay two or three eggs, and skimmers three or four. Most of the eggs in a colony usually hatch within a few days of one another, except where a clutch has been broken up and a female renests. The young chicks (Fig. 40) tend to stay close to the nest site for a while, but some may seek the shelter of a nearby beach plant, or there may be a reshuffling of them due to a disturbance of some sort. When this happens, the chicks may be tended by a different parent.

Fig. 40—Young least (or little) tern trying to hide.

TABLE I
Estimates of Bird Populations, Cobb Island, Virginia, 1875-1931

(from O.L. Austin, Jr., *Bird-Banding*, 1932)

Observers (See Bibliography)	1875 Bailey	1880 Ridgway	1892 Pearson	1901 Kirkwood (in Dutcher)	1902 Andrews (in Dutcher)	1902 Chapman	1903 Andrews (in Dutcher)	1907 Bent	1909 Howell	1930 Hadley	1931 Austin
Laughing Gull	Most abundant		Common	About 1000	About 4000	Several hundred		Abundant	2000	Many hundreds	1200 pairs
Gull-billed Tern			Mentioned	About 1000	About 300	16		4 pairs	16	A few	26 pairs
Caspian Tern		A few	0	0	0	0		0	0	0	0
Royal Tern	A few	1000 pairs	0	0	0	0		0	0	0	0
Forster's Tern	A few (Had not begun to nest)		Considerable number		About 600 (Incl. Common)	Small number		A few (200 prs. on Wreck Isl.)	0	Small colony	437 pairs
Common Tern	Very common		Considerable number	About 200	About 600 (Incl. Forster's)	Several hundred		200 pairs	300	Had not begun to nest	200 pairs
Least Tern	Colonies of 50 pairs a mile apart all along the beach		One seen					0	0	A few	78 pairs
Black Skimmer	Flocks seen (Had not begun to nest)		Large number	About 4000	About 4000	Thousands	New Colony of 1000	Large numbers	300	Many hundreds	1025 pairs
Clapper Rail	Abundant		Considerable number		About 2000			Abundant	Abundant	Common	Common
Willet	Large numbers		5 pairs	2 pairs	4 pairs	2		2	4		4 pairs
Wilson's Plover	12 pairs		Not uncommon	2 pairs	2 pairs	2	30	4	0		8 pairs
Oyster-catcher	6 pairs		Several pairs	12 pairs	4 pairs	2		4	0		4 pairs

Fig. 41—Gull-billed tern with newly hatched chick. This southern species reaches the northern limit of its breeding range in the Middle Atlantic coastal area.

O.S. Pettingill, Jr., observed such reshuffling in a large skimmer colony at Cardwell Island, June 23 to July 6, 1943 (26):

> Although the skimmer chicks wandered away to find shade under various objects, the parent birds I observed do not as a rule join them but return instead to the vicinity of their original nesting sites. This has apparently resulted in certain of the young returning to parents other than their own and being cared for by them. On June 23, I noted one adult brooding two chicks whose ages differed by at least five days. In another, more unusual case I saw an adult skimmer return to its nest which contained three small young, presumably its own. One of them had recently emerged from the egg. Shortly thereafter two more chicks obviously much older, appeared at its side, one following the other. Both crawled beneath the old bird which offered no objection. Because of the noticable difference in ages it was apparent to me that the chicks brooded by these two birds were not in each case hatched from the same set of eggs.

> More extensive observations are necessary to prove conclusively that brooding birds of this species *always* tolerate the presence of young other than their own as these two adults appeared to do; but certainly throughout my hours of watching I saw no attempt on the part of the old birds to prevent their neighbors' chicks from intruding upon their territory nor any evidence of death resulting from attacks by adults.

June to early July is the main part of the nesting season for most local terns and skimmers, but downy young have been seen as late as mid-August.

Because of its unusual method of foraging, several studies have been conducted to determine the skimmers' method of obtaining food. Ivan R. Tomkins (27) says that skimmers feed mostly on low ebb and low flood tides; thus there is about a half-tide cycle when they can feed. They have been known to forage in water as shallow as one inch.

In seeking food, the skimmer tacks back and forth with its lower mandible (lower half of bill or beak) cutting or inserted in the water. The horizontal plane of the body is tilted slightly forward, nearly in line with the long axis of the neck. The birds depress the lower mandible very little. Most of the separation of the mandibles is accomplished by lifting the outer end of the upper mandible as a result of flexing the nasal region.

Richard Zusi (28) observed at one location that skimmers were catching fish at the rate of one fish per bird every three seconds in the course of six minutes of skimming. Of the 115 fish caught, about 15 were dropped, producing an effective catch of one fish per bird per 3.6 seconds.

Erwin (ibid.) lists the following kinds of fish fed to young skimmers in nesting colonies along the coast of Virginia: silversides, killifish, bay anchovy, mullet, spot, and bluefish (See Appendix for scientific names of fish).

Occasionally someone will report what would appear to be a most unusual departure from the usual feeding behavior of terns. On August 20, 1967, Fred Scott noted 25 gull-billed terns feeding in bean fields (probably on insects) near Accomac (29).

Terns and skimmers begin to depart for wintering grounds in late August, however, a few may linger into the fall and even into December. It is rare that a tern or skimmer turns up in a Chincoteague or Cape Charles Christmas Count in late December. Paul Sykes' reporting of 399 Forster's terns at Virginia Beach in December 27, 1967, was most unusual.

Some terns and skimmers winter in the South Atlantic area, particularly along the Florida coast. Two young Forster's terns banded in the Chincoteague Bay area on June 19, 1953, were recovered in the South Atlantic region: one in central Florida on December 13, 1953, and the other in eastern North Carolina on January 2, 1954 (30). But most terns and skimmers seem to winter in the Caribbean. Common terns banded during the nesting season in the Chincoteague Bay area have been recovered in Cuba, Jamaica, the Dominican Republic, Panama, and the northern coast of South America.

Mike Haramis, USFWS

Fig. 42—Adult royal terns at nesting colony on Fisherman's Island near Cape Charles. This southern tern reaches its northern limit in the Chincoteague Bay area a few miles above the Virginia line, where a few have nested on tumps (small islands) in recent years.

Banding Royal Terns at Fisherman's Island

Probably the most extensive banding program of colonial nesting birds of the barrier islands has taken place at the royal tern colony at Fisherman's Island off the tip of Cape Charles (Figs. 43, 45). During some years in the 1960s and 70s, 3-4,000 pairs nested there in tightly-packed colonies. At times there is a spillover of nesting royals to adjacent Smith or other nearby islands. Royal terns (Fig. 44) are near the northern limit of their nesting range along the Virginia coast. Occasionally there are small colonies on

Fig. 43—Royal terns nest in tightly-packed colonies (right), sometimes numbering several thousand pairs.

Fig. 44—Adult royal terns (above) returning to nesting colony with fish for young.

islands in Chincoteague Bay, a few miles north of the Virginia line toward Ocean City, Maryland.

Royal tern colonies are almost always located on islands in densely-packed colonies. According to Buckley and Buckley (31) who have made definitive studies of nesting tern behavior and ecology:

> It is likely that such a high nesting density evolved as a consequence of two major selective pressures: (1) the species' habit of locating its colonies on quadruped-free, bare sand islands near, at or in the middle of inlets, which often forces them to tiny sandbars and shoals with only minimal areas above mean high water suitable for nest sites; and (2) extreme egg predation especially by Laughing Gulls (*Larus atricilla*) on the periphery of the colony. Both these forces should lead to increasing denser colonies, the density eventually peaking when the incubating birds cannot physcially come much closer to each other.

A few pairs of common, little, Sandwich, and gull-billed terns, and piping and Wilson's plovers nest around the periphery of the royal tern colony at Fisherman's Island.

Royal terns arrive at Fisherman's Island in the latter part of March, but do not begin laying their single or occasionally two eggs until the first week in May. Nests, a mere depression in the sand, are so close to one another that it usually is impossible for a person to walk among them without stepping on eggs. At one colony, A.C. Bent (23) counted a hundred nests in four square yards! Eggs generally hatch in late June unless there has been a storm and the colony is washed out. In the event of a washout by storm tides, renesting may take place and hatching may not occur until July, with some young still not old enough to fly until late August.

As of the summer of 1977, nearly 25,000 young royal terns had been banded at the Eastern Shore of Virginia's barrier islands, most of them at Fisherman's Island.

Willet T. Van Velzen and John Weske were among the first ornithologists to band royal tern chicks in large numbers along the Virginia coast. They began operations in 1964. By the middle and late 1970s, Weske was leading banding parties of eight or ten persons at Fisherman's Island that would band up to 3,000 chicks in a few hours. Virtually all of the banding is done on one trip to the

Fig. 45—Typical nesting habitat (right) of royal terns, willets, American oystercatchers and other barrier island nesting birds at Fisherman's Island, Northampton County, Virginia, in 1976. Biologist Woody Martin is rounding up young royal terns to band. Note laughing gulls flying overhead.

Fig. 46—Ornithologist John Weske (top right) and colleagues rounding up and banding royal tern chicks.

Fig. 47—Royal tern chicks (bottom right) driven into corral for banding. As many as 3,000 young terns have been banded in one day at Fisherman's Island.

Mike Haramis, USFWS

Mike Haramis, USFWS

Mike Haramis, USFWS

island, as repeated trips would disturb the colony too much.

Prior to banding, the chicks are herded into a corral (Figs. 46, 47), allowing the mass banding to proceed at a faster pace. It is necessary to band the tern chicks in as short a time as possible because of heat and stress on the young birds.

The largest percentage of recoveries on the wintering grounds are from the eastern and western coasts of Florida, with many scattered throughout the Caribbean Islands and some from Central and South America. Thirty-three recoveries from the Caribbean area were as follows: Dominican Republic, 11; Jamaica, 8; Cuba, 3; French West Indies, 3; Bahamas, 2; Puerto Rico, 2; at sea, 2; Haiti, 1; and Trinidad, 1. Recoveries from Central and South America were from the following locations: Colombia, 5; Honduras, 2; British Honduras, 1; Canal Zone, 1; Venezuela, 1; Guatemala, 1; and Peru, 1.

Van Velzen (32) and Van Velzen and Benedict (33), reporting on recoveries of banded birds, stated that a large number of birds less than one year old winter in Florida and the Caribbean area, and that "Florida recoveries were obtained from November through June, with the high percentage found there during January." Several immatures were found as far south as the Canal Zone and Colombia in May and June, suggesting that birds less than one year old probably do not breed the first season.

There are only a handful of winter records of royal terns wintering along the Eastern Shore of Virginia. One was seen at Chincoteague on December 27, 1951, and on December 30, 1964; there was a record of two at Cape Charles on December 27, 1972.

Shorebirds

More birders go to Chincoteague to see shorebirds than to see the numerous other species. It is one of the best places along the Atlantic Coast to observe various sandpipers, plovers, and allies. Shorebirds offer more surprises than most of the other groups or families of birds that occur

there, and there is the challenge of identifying a number of the smallest shorebird species known as "peeps" (Fig. 48) (least, western, semipalmated, Baird's, and white-

Fig. 48—Semipalmated sandpipers, sometimes known as "peeps," feeding at the edge of the surf. Their foods are mainly mollusks, crustaceans, and other tiny marine organisms. Peeps also include the least, western, white-rumped, and Baird's sandpipers, smallest members of the shorebird family.

rumped sandpipers), which are similar in size and plumage.

Shorebirds are present during every month of the year along the Virginia coast, but those long-distance travellers, many of which nest in the Sub-Arctic and Arctic Tundra and winter in South America are most numerous during migration. The height of spring migration is usually in early May, with thousands still moving through the area during the last week of that month. Black-bellied plovers in their handsome contrasting plumage are the most conspicuous of the migrating shorebirds still present in late May. There is somewhat of a shorebird hiatus from the second week in June to about the second week in July, after which there is a notable influx, with the peak of southward migration in late August. The southbound movement is more protracted than the spring migration, with good flights extending well through September.

Among the less common forms are the curlew sandpiper and the ruff, species that breed in the Old World; the marbled and Hudsonian godwits, and the avocet and

Fig. 49—Ruddy turnstones; the Georgia ornithologist, Ivan Tomkins, describes their habitat as ". . . a firm beach with plenty of shells to be turned over or a jetty with barnacles, or an oysterbed or the groins of the outer beach."

black-necked stilt. More species and rarer forms are being seen today because of the relatively recent establishment of wildlife refuges or sanctuaries along the coastal migration routes of shorebirds, and also because of the much greater number of observers. Some 38 species of shorebirds have been reported at Chincoteague.

Most species of shorebirds occur along the ocean beach (Fig. 49) or mud flats bordering the salt marshes. Some have a decided preference for one habitat over the other.

Fig. 50—Most golden plovers make the southward flight nonstop from the coasts of Labrador or Nova Scotia down over the ocean to the West Indies, and then to Brazil and Argentina. They are uncommon along the Virginia shore.

Bob Hines, USFWS

The sanderling, piping and Wilson's plovers are mainly associated with the ocean beach. The greater and lesser yellowlegs are usually found on the mud flats.

The golden plover (Fig. 50) and upland sandpiper (Fig. 51), birds more closely associated with upland grasslands or prairie-type habitats, are probably more frequent visitors in the Chincoteague area today than formerly because of the extensive lawn-like habitats of Wallop's Island NASA base where some occur during the pause in

Painting by Louis Agassiz Fuertes, Courtesy USFWS

Fig. 51—The upland sandpiper is an uncommon migrant along the Virginia Coastal Strand. It usually occurs on closely-cropped grasslands and frequently perches on fence posts. It occasionally occurs on the ocean beach.

51

their migrations. Occasionally they are seen along the ocean beach. Recent high counts of golden plovers, upland sandpipers and other shorebirds of note are listed in Table II.

Several species of shorebirds nest in the area. One, the willet, is very common in the salt marshes bordering the Chincoteague Causeway where it can be seen at any time from mid-April through the summer. Wilson's and piping plovers (Figs. 52, 53, 54), and the oystercatcher also nest in the area. I noted 12 pairs of Wilson's plovers in a one-half mile stretch on one of the barrier islands below Chincoteague on June 14, 1978.

Although the main southward migration of shorebirds takes place in July, August, and September, there is a continuous and diminishing movement toward the wintering ground throughout the fall. By Christmas in some years, there may still be a surprisingly large number of

sandpipers, plovers, and relatives along the Virginia Coastal Strand. The annual one-day Christmas Counts that take place in late December at Chincoteague and Cape Charles bear this out.

The Purple Sandpiper. Among those hardy wintering shorebirds, one deserves special mention. The purple sandpiper is an exception among the shorebird family as it is near the southern limit of its winter range along the Delmarva coast. It is also the northernmost breeding bird of this group. It nests in Greenland and other islands in the High Arctic and winters from the southern limit of its breeding range southward to the Georgia coast. Where it occurs along the coastal strand, it is usually on the rock jetties that extend out into the ocean. On these jetties, at low tide, it feeds on small organisms that live among the barnacles and kelp.

The Golden Plover. Most of the shorebirds are long-distance migrants, but the golden plover is the champion. The Atlantic form breeds along the Arctic coast from northern Alaska to Baffin Island, and winters on the pampas of Argentina. In migrating from the breeding grounds to the wintering area in South America, golden plovers fly mostly overseas, many from the Labrador coast to the West Indies, and then to the coast of South America, and inland to the pampas or great grasslands of the interior. The few that we see along the coast during fall migration have usually been blown inland by a storm or have wan-

E.O. Mellinger

dered off course. The return journey in the spring is mainly up the Mississippi Valley.

During the five years that I lived on the Grand Prairie in east-central Arkansas, which is in the heart of the Mississippi Flyway, I saw thousands of golden plovers each spring, from late March well into April. During the spring flight they would take their time going north and stop enroute on the Grand Prairie to feed and rest. The earliest birds were still in their complete winter plumage; but six weeks later the last to pass through had completed their prenuptial molt and were in full breeding plumage.

The Whimbrel. This large shorebird with a curved bill is of special interest to birders. As reported by Sprunt and Chamberlain (21), "Their tremendous migrations, pleasing calls, far northern breeding habits, and unusual appearance combine to make them a spectacular species."

Until recent years, the whimbrel was known in bird books as the Hudsonian Curlew, and to the local people as just "curlew," the name they still use. They occur in a wide range of open habitats, but seem to prefer the edge or

Fig. 52—Wilson's plover on nest (left). This southern shorebird reaches the northern limit of its breeding range along the Delmarva Coast.

Fig. 53—Piping plover (right) on nest, Assateague Island, June, 1939.

Fig. 54—Nest and eggs of piping plover (top right) on Assateague Island in June, 1939.

bank of a tidal gut at low tide where they find the greatest number of fiddler crabs, one of their major foods. Most whimbrels winter as far south as Brazil and Chile.

The Eskimo Curlew. The Eskimo curlew (Fig. 55), which apparently has been extinct for some years, probably was always rare along the Delmarva coast. It was more of a migrant of the interior part of the country, particularly the mid-western prairies and Great Plains. Murray (11) placed it on the Virginia hypothetical list. The only evidence on which the bird could be considered for the Virginia list is Rives' report of Captain Crumb's statement that it was a rare and irregular migrant on Cobb's Island. This is very probably correct, as Captain Crumb was a good ornithologist and keen hunter.

53

TABLE II
Recent Summer-Fall Shorebird Records of Note

Species and Number	Locality	Date	Observer
Knot (550)	Chincoteague Ref., Va.	July 14, 1975	B. Williams, et al
Marbled Godwit (52)	Smith Island, Va.	July 16, 1975	B. Williams
Whimbrel (400)	Chincoteague Ref., Va.	July 24, 1976	R.A. Rowlett
Stilt Sandpiper (1,200)	Chincoteague Ref., Va.	July 27, 1974	R.A. Rowlett
Hudsonian Godwit (31)	Chincoteague Ref., Va.	Aug. 10, 1974	L.K. Malone
Upland Sandpiper (46)	Wallops Island, Va.	Aug. 19, 1971	C.R. Vaughn
Lesser Yellowlegs (2,000)	Chincoteague Ref., Va.	Aug. 20, 1974	P. Sykes
Wilson's Phalarope (22)	Chincoteague area, Va.	Aug. 25, 1975	J.M. Abbott, et al
Golden Plover (31)	Wallop's Island, Va.	Sept. 5, 1976	C.R. Vaughn
Buff-breasted Sandpiper (34)	Chincoteague Ref., Va.	Sept. 20, 1974	C.P. Wilds
Sanderling (10,000)	Wallop's Island, Va.	Oct. 5, 1975	C.R. Vaughn
American Avocet (75)	Chincoteague Ref., Va.	Oct. 11, 1971	C.O. Handley, et al
Black-bellied Plover (2,800)	Chincoteague Ref., Va.	Nov. 10, 1974	C.P. Wilds
Dunlin (10,000)	Wallop's Island, Va.	Nov. 22, 1975	C.R. Vaughn

Drawing by Louis Agassiz Fuertes, Courtesy USFWS

Fig. 55—In the course of its migrations between North and South America, the Eskimo curlew became victim of hunters and now apparently is extinct.

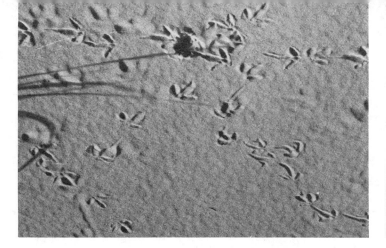

Mike Haramis, USFWS

Luther C. Goldman, USFWS

The Oystercatcher

Ivan Tomkins spent nearly 50 years studying the avifauna of the Savannah River delta along the coast of Georgia. His special interests were the shorebirds, terns, gulls, and other seabirds of the oceanic littoral zone. In one of his published reports (34) he shared some of his sentiments about the oystercatcher and other shorebirds of this dynamic environment:

To one who has lived close to the salt-marsh and the shore, the songs of the shore birds are quite as

Fig. 56—Adult American oystercatcher (right) in familiar surroundings. Four American oystercatchers feeding at oyster bar (above right) at low tide. Chincoteague, January 29, 1978. Oystercatcher tracks (above left) on a sandy beach.

55

harmonious and emotion-waking as the more conventional and better known songs of birds of the field and forest. The barking of the Black Skimmer overhead at night, the plaintive whistle of the Black-bellied Plover, or the wild calls of the Willet in courtship, are full of their particular appeal, but of all the birds I have known, the song of the Oyster-catcher has a special place. The wild pibroch has a cadence and modulation that cannot be described in words. It is one of those things that brings back to mind the 'looming' of winter horizons, the glare of intense sun on barren beach, or storm tides when all the world seems adrift, shutting out the things of every day and opening a remote world. It is a symbol, an actuality and an enigma. The piping of the birds can often be heard a mile away, long before they can be seen. The group sweeps in, wing beats perhaps shortened into the 'butterfly' flight, alights on beach or oyster-reef, choruses and parades with arched necks and bills pointed downward, a performance unique.

The oystercatcher (Fig. 56) has been referred to as the aristocrat of shorebirds. It is one of the largest and certainly one of the handsomest. Its striking black and white plumage, bright red bill, and flesh-colored legs will identify it at a glance. The large white patch in the wings is quite conspicuous in flight (Fig. 57); and its loud call (*kleep!*) will distinguish it from the other birds of the marshes and seabeaches that it inhabits. There are two

Fig. 57—An oystercatcher above the beach circling about its young—and the photographer (far left)—at the south end of Assateague Island. The prominent wing stripe is a good field mark.

Fig. 58—Nest and eggs of American oystercatcher (center left), Wreck Island, Virginia, June, 1947.

Fig. 59—Downy young American oystercatcher (right) standing amid mud snails, Assateague Island, June, 1939.

species in the United States, the American oystercatcher of our Atlantic Coast and the black oystercatcher of the Pacific Coast.

The American oystercatcher occurs during every month of the year at Chincoteague and the Virginia Barrier Islands. It is a very common nesting bird on many of the wild barrier islands. Nesting takes place in May and June. Nest sites (Fig. 58) are on sandy beaches, bare spots in the drier sections of marshes, and sometimes on the fringes of heron and egret nest colonies located on islands in embayments behind the barrier beaches. Two or three eggs are laid in a slight depression in the sand or marsh substrate in May or early June. I have seen small young (Fig. 59) by the first week in June.

In winter, the oystercatcher, black-bellied plover, and the dunlin are the characteristic shorebirds of the coastal strand. In some years, 500 or more oystercatchers are tallied on the one-day Christmas Count at Chincoteague or Cape Charles.

On January 29, 1978, Mike Haramis and I counted 230 American oystercatchers feeding in partly exposed oyster beds in about a one-fourth acre area at Chincoteague. The water was about three inches to four inches in depth. The tide was coming in and apparently the oyster shells were beginning to open as they do when feeding. The birds seemed to have no difficulty in extracting the oysters.

Ivan Tomkins has made the following notes on their feeding behavior (35):

57

They usually feed on 'Raccoon' or 'Coon' oysters, which grow close together, are usually small because of crowding, and usually point upward, in contrast to single oysters, which have more room for growth, are larger, and frequently lie on their sides. Oysters that are feeding, which they do only when covered with water, open the valves slightly, about an eighth of an inch. At other times the valves are held tightly together by the adductor muscle. The slightest touch or jar will usually bring a closing reaction.

Tomkins watched one bird feeding for some time:

It probed the turbid water, apparently finding the oysters by touch rather than by sight. It would probe until (it appeared to me) the bill was entering between the valves of an oyster, press down, repeatedly tip the head from side to side, and soon lift the head with an oyster in plain sight between the mandibles [bill], raising the bill to swallow. If the entire oyster had not been obtained the first time, the oyster-catcher would reach back to get the rest of it. The downward pressure could not have been great, certainly less than the weight of the bird. There was no woodpecker-like hammering, and no sudden thrust. The extreme edge of an oyster shell is very thin and fragile, and it seems that tipping the head sideways allows the bill to fulcrum against one valve and slide inward and downward against the crumbling edge of the other valve. As the head is tipped the other way, the process is reversed. As soon as the bill reaches well in between the valves, the tension on the adductor muscle is released and the flesh of the oyster easily obtained.

Very rarely an oyster clamps down on a bird's beak. Held thus, as in a vise, the bird drowns in the rising tide. Bill Baldwin (36) reported a dead oystercatcher that had its bill caught by a hard-shelled clam, along the South Carolina coast.

While oysters apparently are the oystercatchers' principal food in most areas, they also feed on other marine items. The food habits files of the U.S. Fish and Wildlife Service indicate that bivalves, oysters and clams made up about 95 percent of the food, with marine algae and beetles making up the remainder.

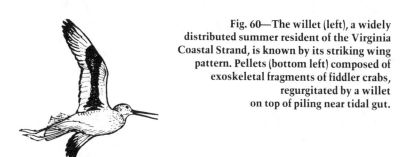

Fig. 60—The willet (left), a widely distributed summer resident of the Virginia Coastal Strand, is known by its striking wing pattern. Pellets (bottom left) composed of exoskeletal fragments of fiddler crabs, regurgitated by a willet on top of piling near tidal gut.

The Willet

In my travels along the South Atlantic and Gulf Coasts, it always seemed to me that the willet (Fig. 60) was more abundant along the Virginia coast than elsewhere in its southern range. It frequents a variety of habitats, but is primarily associated with the salt marsh.

It is well known because of its pronounced calls, its white wing patch, prominently displayed when in flight, and its habit of perching on man-made structures. It is the only shorebird in the area that regularly perches on pil-

Fig. 61—Nest and eggs of willet (top right) on Virginia Barrier Island beach, June 14, 1978. Willet nest and eggs in salt-marsh meadow (bottom right), Chincoteague, June 3, 1977.

Fig. 62—The willet is essentially a bird of the salt marsh and barrier beach, but frequently perches on man-made objects such as posts, signs, and telephone wires.

ings, dead trees, railings, signs (Fig. 62), telephone wires, and the like. The upland sandpiper, an uncommon migrant along the coast, does the same on its breeding ground, which is farther inland and mostly north of the Eastern Shore of Virginia.

The willet gets its common name from its shrill call, *pull-will-willet*; and its scientific name *Catoptrophorus*, a Greek term meaning "carrying a mirror," from its white wing patch.

Willets are spring and summer residents that arrive on the Virginia coast in April. Many of them nest in the salt meadows where the dense *Spartina patens* grass conceals the eggs or beside a tuft of grass on the seabeach, in heronries beside a bush, and sometimes along the side of a road where, whenever a person walks by, the incubating bird flushes from its nest. I recall the time I was walking

in a straight line along the center of Metomkin Island, which is almost entirely seabeach, and flushed five willets from their nests within a distance of 200 feet (Fig. 61).

Like the clapper rail, boat-tailed grackle, and some other birds that spend most of their time in or near the salt marshes, willets feed to a great extent on fiddler crabs. I have seen the exoskeleton material of these crustaceans that was regurgitated by willets in the form of pellets and deposited on the tops of pilings.

This most ubiquitous of shorebirds along the Virginia coast during the summer half of the year departs on its southward journey by early fall. A few are recorded on some Christmas Counts in late December, but these may be late migrants that are lagging behind in their flight to wintering grounds in the tropics. I seldom see one in January along the Virginia Coastal Strand.

Herons, Ibises, and Egrets

Fig. 63—Snowy egret (right) forages for minnows, crustaceans, and other aquatic animal life and is a common summer resident, nesting in mixed heron-egret-glossy ibis colonies.

Fig. 64—The Louisiana heron (far right) is a common breeding bird along the Virginia Coastal Strand.

Fig. 65—The glossy ibis (below), a southern species, is now a common summer resident, nesting in colonies with herons and egrets.

John W. Taylor

The coastal strand of Virginia's Eastern Shore, because of its chain of relatively isolated barrier islands, and smaller natural and spoil-dredge islands in nearby embayments, has for at least the last fifty years been one of the best established nesting grounds for herons and egrets along the Atlantic coast. By 1956, glossy ibises from the south began moving into the area to nest in some of the Virginia and Maryland coastal heronries; and in 1977 the first pair of nesting white ibises was reported in a mixed heron-egret nesting colony along the Virginia coast (37). The white ibis nest was located in a heronry at the tip end of the peninsula, at Fisherman's Island.

Most of the same Virginia coastal heronries are used year after year. Northward from the coast of Virginia, heronries become fewer and more tenuous. In addition to

Fig. 66—Glossy ibises over nesting colony.

Fig. 67—Herons and egrets over tops of high-tide bush (*Iva*) nesting colony near Gargathy Bay, June 14, 1978. Nesting species include little blue, Louisiana, and black-crowned night herons; great, snowy, and cattle egrets; and glossy ibises.

the many optimum sites for nesting and foraging, a major factor in the success of heronries in coastal Virginia has been freedom from disturbance, a condition not often met farther north where the coastal strip is densely peopled because of resorts and industry.

Most heronries or rookeries in this area are composed of mixed species which include the following: great egret, snowy egret (Fig. 63), cattle egret, little blue heron, Louisiana heron (Fig. 64, 67a), black-crowned night heron, glossy ibis (Figs. 65, 66) and occasionally green heron and yellow-crowned night heron (*See* Table III).

The cattle egret, like the glossy ibis, is a relatively recent "invader" of nesting colonies of the Delmarva Peninsula. The first nesting record of the cattle egret in the area was in 1957, at Mills Island, located in the Maryland section of Chincoteague Bay, a few miles north of the Virginia boundary. Since that time nesting cattle egrets have increased to the point where they could possibly pose a problem for herons and other egrets as sometimes they are competitive in seeking nest sites in a heronry. Also, they usually begin nesting later than some of the herons and egrets and sometimes rob sticks from active nests to be used in the construction of their own. The sticks are taken from the nests of other large waders when they are out gathering food for their young or during the egg-laying period when adults may be out foraging for themselves. If too many sticks are taken by the cattle egrets, eggs or young may fall out of the often flimsy nests. So far, cattle egrets do not seem to be much of a problem in the heronries I have visited.

Fig. 67b—Two Louisiana herons standing in center and one, to the left, landing; white birds on the right are cattle egrets, at heronry rookery near Chincoteague, June 18, 1979.

The cattle egret is a recent immigrant to North America. It was originally a native bird of Africa. Some migrated across the Atlantic to South America in about 1930. Having become established in the southern hemisphere, it then "invaded" North America, and was first observed in this country in Florida in about 1941; the first reported nesting in that state was in 1953. As far as I can ascertain, the first coastal Virginia record was made by John Buckalew on May 13, 1953.

It has adapted so well that it is now one of the most abundant large waders in the United States. As pointed out by Valentine (38):

> The presence of already established heronries is probably an important factor in the rapid spread of the Cattle Egret. All of the known Cattle Egret nesting colonies in the United States are within the confines of established egret and heron nesting sites.

The northward extension of the breeding range of the glossy ibis is also quite remarkable. Prior to the 1940s in the Atlantic coastal area they were known to breed only in Florida. By the 1940s the breeding range had been

Fig. 68—Great egrets in nesting colony.

Fig. 69—Nest and pale-blue eggs of snowy egrets showing nesting density in heronry or rookery near Chincoteague, May 28, 1978. Of the many nearby nests, some belonged to Louisiana herons and cattle egrets, most were 2 to 4 feet from the ground.

Peter J. Van Huizen

TABLE III   Breeding Population Estimates of Herons, Egrets, and Ibises

There are a number of heron-egret-ibis nesting colonies along the Virginia Coastal Strand. Population estimates of several are as follows:

a) In 1975, Mitchell Byrd reported 2,775 nesting pairs of large waders of several species at Parramore Island; 1,200 were glossy ibises (from *American Birds*).

b) In 1976, Mitchell Byrd reported 1,175 pairs of black-crowned night herons in a mixed colony of large waders at Fisherman's Island (from *American Birds*).

c) Wire Narrows, Chincoteague Bay, May 28, 1978 (Buckalew and Meanley):
   snowy egret (125 pairs)   little blue heron (50)
   cattle egret (100)   great egret (50)
   Louisiana heron (100)   glossy ibis (25)
        black-crowned night heron (20)

d) Gargathy Bay, June 14, 1978 (Taylor and Meanley):
   Louisiana heron (50 pairs)   great egret (20)
   snowy egret (40)   cattle egret (15)
   glossy ibis (30)   little blue heron (15)
        black-crowned night heron (2)

e) In 1958, Jacob Valentine reported the composition of a heronry at Mill's Island, Chincoteague Bay, (from the *Raven*):
   snowy egret (200 pairs)   Louisiana heron (30)
   black-crowned night heron (50)   little blue heron (30)
   great egret (40)   glossy ibis (25)
        cattle egret (12)

Fig. 70—Young great egrets nearly ready to leave their nest.

extended northward to the Carolinas, by the mid-1950s to the Middle Atlantic coast, and now north to Maine. Bill Williams (39), who has studied glossy ibises at Wachapreague for several years, seems to have a reasonable explanation for the northward range extension of this species. Young glossy ibises have fledged by mid-July, and tend to wander north for a few weeks before migrating in early fall to southern wintering grounds. To quote Williams:

It is not hard to imagine, then that in subsequent years as the birds mature they will return to these areas encountered as immatures that were favorable and establish nesting sites, especially where herons and egrets have colonized in previous seasons.

A white ibis immigration also appears to be developing. In addition to the first Virginia nest in 1977, there were sightings of adult white ibises at two other locations along the Virginia coast that year.

Egrets, herons, and ibises at this latitude are mainly birds of the summer-half of the year. Relatively few winter this far north as indicated by the Chincoteague and Cape Charles Christmas Counts that take place in late December each year.

They arrive on their breeding grounds beginning in late March and early April. The usual nesting sites of the colonies are in low bushes, usually high-tide bush (*Iva*) (Figs. 67b, 68). This is the vegetation that covers parts of some of the islands in the embayments. Most of these islands are small, often less than an acre in size, and in addition to being packed with nesting herons, egrets, and ibises, may also have many nests of boat-tailed grackles, and on the ground along the edges of some heronries, scattered nests of laughing and herring gulls, a few terns, willets, and oystercatchers. Occasionally a heronry is located in cedars or pines on one of the isolated barrier islands.

Nest building begins in April. Since the principal nest sites are bushes, usually not much more than eight feet in height, nests are necessarily placed only about two to four feet from the ground. This makes it convenient for bird banders. By contrast, many heronries in southern swamps are often well near the tops of cypress trees, sometimes 50 or 60 feet from the ground. Those herons and egrets that nest in cedar trees on Virginia Barrier Islands and on Mills Island in Chincoteague Bay, may have their structures 20 feet or so up in the trees.

A few early nesters have laid eggs by the first week in May; the peak of laying is usually in the latter part of that month. When John Buckalew and I visited the Wire Narrows heronry near Chincoteague on May 28, 1978, most of the clutches were incomplete, with one to three eggs of the usual four egg clutch (Fig. 69). Most of the glossy ibises had full clutches of four eggs (Fig. 71). The herons and egrets have pale blue eggs and the glossy ibises a deeper bluish-green egg. Glossy ibises tend to nest in

groups, but with an occasional heron or egret nest mixed among theirs. The various species of herons and egrets tend to nest separately, but there is nearly always some mixing. Some nests in heronries on the Eastern Shore of the Virginia coast are only a foot from the ground; many nests are just two or three feet apart. Snowy egret, little blue heron and Louisiana heron nests are made almost entirely of sticks, but the glossy ibis uses some grass for lining its stick nest; the great egret sometimes makes a comparatively well constructed nest of sticks and grass.

Young (Figs. 70, 72) fledge (leave the nest) mainly in July, with a few fledging up until late August. Jacob Valentine found three active nests as late as August 23, 1958.

Williams (ibid.) has suggested that ibises are compatible with herons and egrets in nesting colonies and environs because they occupy a slightly different niche in their nesting and feeding habits. At a Wachapreague colony, snowy egrets and Louisiana herons nested higher in the bushes and more on the branches of such, while the ibises nested lower and close to the trunk. Food fed to young herons and egrets was mainly minnows; food of nestling ibises was mainly insect larvae and crustaceans.

Herons, egrets, and ibises obtain their food mostly from brackish and salt marsh ponds, and freshwater impoundments; but the cattle egret is an exception, feeding mostly in pastures where it associates with the Chincoteague ponies, and at nearby cattle ranches. In its original home, in Africa, it has always been known to feed with the ungulates or larger hoofed animals, especially in the presence of the water buffalo. They feed on terrestrial insects, especially grasshoppers, also on spiders, and amphibians that are flushed by the cattle or ponies as these large mammals stroll along. They also pick horseflies off the legs and belly and back of these animals. They frequently perch on the back of cattle, which usually do not seem to mind. I have seen a cow asleep with a cattle egret perched on its back that was also asleep.

Most herons, egrets, and ibises depart for the wintering grounds in September and October, but a few winter along the Virginia Coastal Strand. Many of these large waders winter in the Caribbean area and along the coasts of Central and South America. Vernon Kleen reported (22), the following recoveries of large waders that he and David Bridge banded at heronries on islands in Chincoteague Bay:

- Little blue heron—banded June 9, 1962, recovered in Trinite, Martinique, French West Indies, September 22, 1962.

- Great egret—banded June 11, 1961, recovered in Grand Bahamas, British West Indies, January 27, 1964.

- Louisiana heron—banded July 28, 1962, recovered in Oropoli, Honduras, January 3, 1963.

Also, several Louisiana herons banded in Wachapreague were recovered in Ecuador and Haiti.

The great blue heron, one of the most common of all large waders and certainly the hardiest, is a rather uncommon breeding bird of the Virginia coast. Most of them nest farther inland along tidewater, particularly in the Chesapeake Bay area. But it is usually the most common winter resident of the heron-egret group in the area. On the December 27, 1975, Christmas Count at Chincoteague, 303 were reported. On the same count there were 215 great egrets, 139 black-crowned night herons, 109 snowy egrets, 132 Louisiana herons, 2 yellow-crowned night herons, and 27 glossy ibises.

Fig. 72—Young glossy ibises in heron-egret-ibis nesting colony near Gargathy Bay, June 14, 1978. Note the three black bands on the bill; these are not present in the adult.

The Herring Gull — A New Nesting Bird in Virginia

John W. Taylor

Fig. 73—The herring gull, winter resident, has in recent years become a fairly common breeding bird. Nearly 200 pairs nested near Chincoteague, May - June, 1978.

When J.J. Murray's *Check-List of the Birds of Virginia* was published in 1952, there were no records of the nesting of the herring gull (Fig. 73) in the state. Now this large gull has extended its breeding range southward from New England, and is a fairly common nesting bird in some of the Virginia coastal marshes. There are nesting colonies of several hundred pairs in some sections, a few small groups of a dozen or so birds in others, and single pairs scattered about. One nest that I saw in May, 1978, was located adjacent to a heron-egret-ibis nesting colony. In the Chincoteague area I would call it a common breeding bird. At Hog Island on June 18, 1976,

Fig. 74—Ornithologist John H. Buckalew (left) at nest site of herring gull in salt-meadow cordgrass (*Spartina patens*), Chincoteague, May 27, 1978. Buckalew observing herring gull's nesting habitat (above). Closeup of herring gull nest and eggs (right) in salt-meadow cordgrass.

Mitchell Byrd and Bill Williams found 650 nesting pairs.

If the herring gull breeding population continues to increase along the Virginia coast, there eventually may be competition with the smaller laughing gull. Herring gulls usually nest in higher parts of a marsh than do laughing gulls; but colonies of the two species are often close together. A typical herring gull nesting habitat is a mixture of high-tide bush and salt-meadow cordgrass (Fig. 74). The laughing gull's traditional nest site is usu-ally in the lower salt-marsh cordgrass nearer the tidal creeks; a few sometimes nest in the slightly higher salt-meadow cordgrass if it is close to a tidal creek. Both species sometimes nest on the grassy sections of barrier beaches.

At present the laughing gull seems not only to be holding its own but is perhaps increasing in the Virginia coastal area.

The Herring Gull's Midden

A highly adaptable species, the herring gull is consequently one of the most abundant and widely distributed seabirds of the Northern Hemisphere. Subsisting on a wide range of foods, it is a scavenger that forages around harbors, garbage dumps, or a hundred miles at sea on the offal discarded by fishing vessels. Gulls have been known to follow ships all the way across the ocean, feeding on scraps tossed overboard along the way. Fin- and shellfish

Fig. 75—A half-sunken barge littered with broken clam shells near Chincoteague . The bits of shells are the result of herring gulls dropping clams from a height of 20 to 30 feet so that these hard-shelled mollusks will break upon impact.

also furnish a large part of the herring gull's diet, and their methods of handling shellfish are particularly interesting. A.C. Bent (23) describes methods used by gulls in dismantling mollusks and crustaceans:

> Many crabs and mollusks are broken with the bill, but if this can not be accomplished the gull seizes the difficult morsel and flies up with it into the air, nearly vertically or in circles, drops it onto the hard sand or rocks, follows closely the descent, and alights to regale itself on the exposed contents. If unsuccessful the first time the gull tries a second and sometimes a third or fourth time. This habit, which is also a common one with crows, explains the fact that mollusk shells, crabs, and sea urchins are scattered so universally along our coast, sometimes half a mile from the sea.

At numerous times along the Virginia coast I have seen a herring gull pick up a clam at low tide, rise 20 or 30 feet in the air, and drop it on a wooden bridge, hardtop road, or pile of oyster shells. I have seen the surface of a wooden bridge that was seldom used, covered completely with broken clam shells. At Chincoteague, in the spring of 1978, John Taylor and I saw a half sunken barge in a tidal gut that had become a herring gull's midden (Fig. 75); and nearby we observed gulls catching spider crabs (Fig. 76) and dropping them from a considerable height on oyster shell mounds to immobilize them and crack the shell.

Fig. 76—The spider crab (*Libinia emarginata*) is one of the many kinds of foods of herring gulls that forage in Chincoteague Bay. The gulls take them also up in the air and drop them on a hard surface to immobolize them and crack their shell.

73

The Boat-Tailed Grackle

The boat-tailed grackle (Fig. 77), like the gull-billed, royal, and Sandwich terns, the Wilson's plover, chuck-will's-widow, and brown-headed nuthatch, is a southern bird that reaches the northern limit of its breeding range along the Middle Atlantic Coast. A few boat-tails are found as far north as the coast of southern New Jersey, but from Chincoteague southward along the coast they are a common and much more conspicuous bird, particularly along the salt marshes. A few are found in the Chesapeake Bay

Fig. 77—Adult male boat-tailed grackle (right), known locally as the "jackdaw," is essentially a salt marsh bird.

Fig. 78—Male boat-tailed grackle (upper right) in courtship flight over nesting grounds. As it displays before a female grackle, its throat is puffed out, tail is V-shaped, and its flight is like a butterfly's. Nest of boat-tailed grackle in top of center bush in heron-egret-ibis nesting colony (lower right); there were three eggs in the nest.

country as far north as Elliott and Hooper Islands; in some years sizeable nesting colonies are located near the village of Elliott in Dorchester County, Maryland.

The boat-tail's name comes from its long keel-shaped tail, which is more prominently boat-shaped during the courtship period when the male is in flight (Fig. 78). However, the boat-tail is better known locally as "Jackdaw." Along the southwest Louisiana coast where I worked for several years, the Cajun rice farmers call this bird "Chock."

The adult male boat-tailed grackle has a brilliant metallic bluish black plumage, and is nearly as long (15-17 inches) as a crow, but weighs considerably less; nearly two-thirds of its length is its tail. The smaller female (about 12 inches) is attired in sepia brown above and buffy tan below.

Boat-tailed grackles nest in colonies of their own or in heronries on islands where their nests are mixed among those of the various species of herons, egrets, and the glossy ibis. In such colonies their nests of salt-marsh grasses and mud (Fig. 79) are usually placed in high-tide bushes and wax myrtle, often only three or four feet above the ground.

They feed mainly on fiddler crabs, small blue crabs, and other crustaceans, fish, and insects; they are also scavengers coming into towns like Chincoteague, Wachapreague, and Oyster to feed on scraps of food. Sometimes they flock together with red-winged blackbirds and the smaller common grackle in raiding cornfields located near the coast.

Mike Haramis, USFWS

Apparently little is known about their migration. There seem to be almost as many around the Virginia coast in winter as in summer. Indications are that there is some permanent residency and only slight shifting coastwise. The following recoveries support this view:

- Banded, coast of Maryland, June 30, 1962; recovered, coast of Virginia, December, 1965.
- Banded, coast of Maryland, June 15, 1963; recovered, coast of Maryland, October, 1963.
- Banded, coast of Virginia, June 9, 1966; recovered, coast of Virginia, January 27, 1969.
- Banded, coast of Virginia, May 26, 1967; recovered, coast of Virginia, December 29, 1973.
- Banded, coast of Maryland, June 10, 1961; recovered, coast of New Jersey, May 14, 1973.

Fig. 79—Nest and eggs of boat-tailed grackle in wax myrtle bush. This large coastal grackle nests in colonies close to the marshes, its principal feeding area.

The Breeding Birds of the Maritime Loblolly Pine Forest

Some of the barrier islands have fairly extensive stands of loblolly pines. Assateague, Parramore Islands, and Chincoteague, which lies behind Assateague, have the best pine forests (Fig. 80). Some of these pine stands have an undergrowth of hardwood saplings, mainly oaks and gums, mixed with American holly, wax myrtle bushes, and greenbrier jungles. Large water oaks, a southern species near the northern limit of its range, grows in the more open areas of the pinewoods belt on Assateague.

Fig. 80—Assateague Light is surrounded mostly by loblolly pinewoods and a few hardwoods. Other than being a nesting area, various species of small birds move through the pine forests en route to wintering grounds in the tropics.

The breeding and wintering birds of these island forests are the same as those on the mainland. During periods of migration, particularly in the fall, local pineland bird populations are augmented by large numbers of songbirds from northern breeding grounds en route to wintering areas in the tropics.

Fig. 81—Adult brown-headed nuthatch (below) with spider in bill — perched beside nesting hole in dead snag. Parent birds like these keep busy to provide their young with the food they need.

Fig. 82—Tree swallow (above) standing at entrance to its nest cavity in dead pine stub. Like many hole-nesting species they often choose old woodpecker holes in pine stubs. Nests are lined with feathers, usually those of waterfowl, found in the flotsam or windrows along the edge of a marsh; their eggs are white. The Virginia coast is the southern limit of their nesting range.

The loblolly pine (*Pinus taeda*) is a southern tree that reaches its northern limit on the Delmarva Peninsula. The more moderate climate along the coast and the sandy soils are the principal reason that its range extends to southern Delaware. It is of special interest that the northern limit of the breeding range of both the brown-headed

Fig. 83—Young ospreys (right) in nest made of sticks, boards, clods of earth from a marsh, and dead submerged aquatic plants (seaweed). Nests are placed in dead pine trees, channel markers and other man-made objects, and occasionally on the ground on uninhabited islands. Coastal strand (below) showing low growth of loblolly pines, high-tide bushes, and large dead pines with osprey nests.

nuthatch and chuck-will's-widow coincides with that of the loblolly pine.

The variety of birds is greater in the maritime loblolly pine forest near tidewater than in such pine stands of the interior of the Delmarva Peninsula, which are usually denser. The greater variety of nesting species in pinelands near the water is due to the thinner stands and to the much greater number of dead pine stubs, remnants of pines that have succumbed to saturation or too much inundation from the tides. Thus there are many more nest sites for hole-nesting species like the brown-headed nuthatch (Fig. 81), tree swallow (Fig. 82), house wren, crested flycatcher, Carolina chickadee, tufted titmouse, eastern bluebird, and several species of woodpeckers. Sometimes two or three species will be nesting at the same time in the same dead pine stub.

Birds that nest in live pines along the coastal strand include the pine warbler, blue-gray gnatcatcher, orchard oriole, boat-tailed grackle, common grackle, blue jay, summer tanager, chipping sparrow, mockingbird, eastern wood pewee, eastern kingbird, mourning dove, ruby-throated hummingbird, great horned owl, common crow, fish crow, and osprey.

In 1875, H. Bailey (40) reported that 50 pairs of ospreys nested on Hog Island. Most of the nests were in dead pines. Two nests were on the ground. He found the nest of an osprey and fish crow in the same tree. Osprey nests (Fig. 83) are still a fairly common sight along the Virginia coast.

At Cedar Island, John Buckalew found a pile of over 100 eggshells lying beneath the pine-tree feeding perch of a fish crow, a bird well known for its pilfering of birds' nests. The eggs were chiefly those of laughing gulls, clapper rails, red-winged blackbirds, boat-tailed grackles, willets, and herons.

A number of species are associated with the heavy undergrowth of sections of the pine forest. Common nesting birds include the cardinal, gray catbird, rufous-sided towhee, Carolina wren, brown thrasher, and white-eyed vireo. Most of these species, in fewer numbers, also occur there regularly in winter. The white-eyed vireo is an exception. White-throated and fox sparrows and several other species from the North also winter in the undergrowth.

A more complete picture of the avifauna of the loblolly pinewoods in the Chincoteague area in winter can be obtained from Christmas Counts that occur there each year (See Appendix I). Some notable counts of pinewoods birds observed on the December, 1975, Christmas Count were as follows: red-breasted nuthatch 194, brown-headed nuthatch 215, golden-crowned kinglet 444, ruby-crowned kinglet 226, pine warbler 15, and red crossbill 107.

The only record of the rather rare red-cockaded woodpecker in the Chincoteague area was of a bird that I saw just a short distance above the Virginia line on Assateague Island, June 9, 1939 (41).

John W. Taylor

The Peregrine Falcon

Each autumn, usually from late September to early October, the Eastern States highest concentration of peregrine falcons (Fig. 84) still pass along the Virginia Coastal Strand en route to wintering grounds in the West Indies and South America. Most of them come from breeding grounds along the Labrador and Greenland coasts and the Arctic coast of Canada.

This spectacular bird of prey that once nested regularly on cliffs of nearby Virginia, Maryland, and Pennsylvania mountains, is now on the rare and endangered list, and today nests nowhere in the eastern United States. As far as I can ascertain, the last active nest in Virginia was in the early 1950s.

Between September 25 and October 16, 1970, F.P. Ward and R.B. Berry (42) counted 68 peregrines along the beach and sand dune area at Assateague, and a year later, 120 in the same general area.

Fig. 84—The northeastern population
of the Peregrine falcon migrates
along the Virginia Barrier Islands en route to
wintering grounds in the tropics.
Some come from as far away as Greenland.

Most of the peregrines migrate along the ocean beaches where they prey on shorebirds and other migrants following the coastline southward. A few peregrines are captured by falconers who enjoy the ancient sport of falconry that for centuries has been a favorite pastime of noblemen in various parts of the world. Only a few qualified persons are licensed to obtain falcons for the purpose of training and flying them.

One of the methods of obtaining falcons along the ocean beach is unique. Working as a team, falconers drive along the beach until they see a bird; and then one member of the team buries the other in the sand, except for his head and hands. A box with a slit in it or a wire basket interwoven with beach grass is placed over his head. Lying in this supine position and covered with sand he no longer looks like a human being to a peregrine falcon. In this position he holds a pigeon in his hands, awaiting the arrival of the peregrine. The falcon soon sights the lure and attacks. Shortly after it alights on its prey, the man in the sand just has to move his hands slightly and slowly around a leg of the falcon and hold tight.

Most falcons that are trapped are banded and released. Two peregrines banded at Assateague Island were later captured on the west coast of Greenland. One banded in Greenland was recovered in Cuba.

Fig. 85—Worm-eating warbler (left) caught in a mist net — method used to intercept migrating songbirds for banding and recording of other data during Operation Recovery at Kiptopeke. In late September (below), bird bander removing redstart from mist net at Kiptopeke.

Operation Recovery at Kiptopeke

Since 1963 an annual early autumn songbird banding program (Fig. 85) has been conducted by members of the Virginia Ornithological Society at Kiptopeke, near the southern terminus of the Eastern Shore peninsula. The

mist-netting project is part of a cooperative banding study along the Atlantic Coast known as Operation Recovery. The primary purpose of the program is to study the distribution and migration of birds, and to correlate bird movements with various weather phenomena.

Kiptopeke is a key station in the Operation Recovery program because it is located where the peninsula tapers down to a point, having the effect of funneling birds into a narrow passageway, thus concentrating a wide variety and large number into a relatively small area. The banding station is operated during the height of the southward migration of songbirds, which is mainly in September and October. As many as 80 persons work at the station at one time or another, removing birds from the finely-meshed Japanese mist nets, weighing, measuring, sexing, aging, and determining body fat, and then banding and releasing the birds. Frederic R. Scott, prominent Virginia ornithologist and editor of the *Raven*, journal of the Virginia Society of Ornithology, initiated the project and he is still the guiding genius.

As many as 30 or 40 mist nets are strategically placed in lanes next to hedgerows and along woods borders. Each net is 40 feet in length and seven feet in height.

The results of the netting or recovery program are highly dependent on weather. Best conditions are a northwest wind following the passage of a strong cold front. Under these conditions, so many birds may be intercepted that it is often necessary to take some of the nets out of operation in order to handle the deluge. However, as such cold fronts are generally predicted ahead of time, there are usually enough birders to cope with the situation.

The participating banders have an extraordinary opportunity to become better acquainted with birds in their fall plumages. Following the postnuptial and post-juvenal molts of birds in summer, warblers in particular, of which there are so many species, and which have such brilliant plumages during the breeding season in spring, have now assumed a drab plumage. (In technical parlance, juvenal refers to the plumage of a young bird, and juvenile to the young bird itself). One often has to turn to the familiar field guides and refer to plates depicting warblers in their confusing fall plumage.

As many as 13,000 birds representing nearly 100 species have been intercepted and banded in a two-month operation at Kiptopeke. The Swainson's thrush, gray-cheeked thrush, American redstart, gray catbird, myrtle or yellow-rumped warbler, yellowthroat, and red-eyed vireo are usually in the top 10 of the most birds caught each fall.

Birds banded at Operation Recovery stations along the New England and New Jersey coasts and elsewhere have been recovered at Kiptopeke, and several banded at the Virginia station have been recovered at distant locations. The following recovery information is based on data mainly from the *Raven*, 1968, 1970, 1972, and the *North American Bird Bander*, 1977:

Fig. 86—This Swainson's warbler was recaptured in a Japanese mist net in an eastern Virginia swamp within 20 feet of where it had been banded a year earlier. The several dozen licensed bird banders in Delmarva are experienced ornithologists, required to have state and federal banding permits.

- A northern waterthrush banded at Lincoln, Massachusetts, September 15, 1969, was recovered at Kiptopeke eight days later, September 23.
- A Swainson's thrush banded at Ocean City, Maryland, September 23, 1967, was recaptured the following day at Kiptopeke, about 95 miles to the south.
- A blackpoll warbler banded at Willoughby, Ohio, September 17, 1975, was recovered at Kiptopeke, October 24, 1975.
- Two sharp-shinned hawks banded at Cape May, New Jersey, October 6 and 21, 1975, were recovered at Kiptopeke, October 20 and 24, 1975.
- A sharp-shinned hawk banded at Kiptopeke, October 15, 1975, was recovered in April, 1976, at Lac Megantic, Quebec.

Also, a number of birds beyond their normal range or somewhat off course were captured at the Virginia station. A black-headed grosbeak, a western bird captured at the station on October 16, 1971, was the third record of that species for the state of Virginia. A Swainson's warbler (Fig. 86) caught on September 12, 1971, was the first record of the species for the Eastern Shore of Virginia.

The Operation Recovery station at Kiptopeke is not operated in the spring since at that time of the year the migration of songbirds is not as heavy along the coast. The larger percentage of thrushes, vireos, and warblers migrate farther inland at that season, along the Inner Coastal Plain, Piedmont and mountain provinces.

The Ipswich Sparrow

One of the interesting aspects of bird distribution concerns the unusual and highly restricted ranges of some species. One of the best known examples of a bird with a limited range in the coastal area is the Ipswich sparrow (Fig. 87). This pale colored bird of the sand dunes is known as the bird with a range "a thousand miles long and a hundred yards wide." During the winter it is found along the Atlantic coastal sand dunes from Nova Scotia (where only a few of them winter) into Georgia, and rarely as far south as Florida. During the breeding season it nests only on Sable Island off the coast of Nova Scotia.

The Ipswich sparrow was discovered in 1868 by C.J. Maynard on a dune beach at Ipswich, Massachusetts. Many years earlier, Alexander Wilson, one of our foremost pioneer ornithologists, obtained a specimen on a New Jersey beach, and thinking that it was an adult male Savannah sparrow, figured it under that name in his monumental *American Ornithology*, published between 1808-1814.

This pale sparrow of the dunes is nowhere common along its coastal winter range. It does not occur in flocks like some sparrows, although occasionally two or three

Gorman M. Bond

Fig. 87—The Ipswich sparrow is found only along Atlantic coastal sand dunes and beaches. Here it is perched on the twig of a beach plum.

may be seen feeding together on the seeds of a single dune plant. Several of these sparrows sometimes occur in company with small flocks of snow buntings and horned larks, which frequent the dunes from time to time, as well as other habitats.

According to ornithologists Stobo and McLarin, who have written a monograph (43) on this sparrow, "Their abundance at a given latitude is related to plant cover, relief, and freshwater." Little catch basins or ponds of rainwater occur here and there on the back side of dunes or in the trough between dunes.

Although distributed along the seashore from Halifax, Nova Scotia, to Jacksonville, Florida, in winter, the center of abundance at that season is the Delmarva coast. The earliest birds usually arrive along the barrier islands of Virginia by the first week in November; the latest departures are by mid-April. Highest counts in one day at Assateague Island seldom exceed 25-30 birds.

The Ipswich sparrow is one of a small number of birds that is truly unique. But alas, *Passerculus princeps* no longer holds the rank of a full species, a position it held from 1868, when it was described by ornithologist C.J. Maynard, until 1973, when it was "lumped" taxonomically with the closely related Savannah sparrow (*Passerculus sandwichensis*), and thus was relegated to subspecific status, now being known as a geographic race or variety of the abundant and widespread Savannah. Thus it has become *Passerculus sandwichensis princeps*, even though it averages about 10 percent larger and is considerably lighter or paler than the Savannah sparrow.

All of this came about in 1973 when the Committee for the Check-List of North American Birds of the American Ornithologists' Union, a panel of scientists that periodically reviews the status of closely related birds, decided that since the Ipswich and Savannah are closely allied morphologically and occasionally interbreed in Nova Scotia where their ranges overlap, they should be considered a single species or two subspecies of the same species.

An example of a recent change in the status of two well known species that have been lumped are the Baltimore oriole of the east and Bullock's oriole of the west. The plumage and other morphological aspects are similar, and they have been found to interbreed where their ranges overlap in the Great Plains.

Most Savannah sparrows that breed in Nova Scotia are found on the mainland, but occasionally a handful wander over to Sable Island where they have been found mated with the Ipswich, and very rarely the same interbreeding may occur when a stray Ipswich visits the nearby mainland.

So in the end, Alexander Wilson who pictured the Ipswich sparrow in his *American Ornithology* and labeled it a Savannah sparrow, was about 170 years ahead of todays' modern scientist, although he did not realize his "mistake" at the time!

The Christmas Bird Count

Begun at Chincoteague in 1952 and at Cape Charles in 1965, the Christmas Bird Count has been an annual event ever since (*See* Appendix I for list of species and highest counts at Chincoteague and Cape Charles).

For one day or one 24-hour period, usually during Christmas week (December 25-January 1), birders assemble at these and other places to count the number of species and individuals of each species in designated areas. The area is the same 15-mile circle each year.

The Christmas Bird Count is sponsored by the National Audubon Society, and has been a nationwide event since 1900. The first year there were 25 counts in the United States. By the 1970s, there were over 1,000 counts in North America, with some 20,000 participants. The main purpose of the Christmas Counts is to note population trends and changes in distribution patterns of birds.

Participants look forward to returning to a favorite birding spot and spending a day in the field with friends who have a common interest. They come to the area expecting to see something unusual, so there is the challenge to go and seek it out. The competition between different Christmas Count areas is keen.

Coastal areas are especially productive, and consequently register the greatest number of species. In 1975, Chincoteague had 172 species and Cape Charles 170. In the same year in the mountain region of Virginia, the Peaks of Otter and Big Flat Mountain each had 34 species.

In most years the number of species counted at Chincoteague and Cape Charles is greater than at other points along the Middle Atlantic Coast, as well as the New England coast. Usually, the farther south one moves along the coast toward Florida, the higher the counts.

The average number of species recorded at Cape Charles during the 10-year period 1967-1976 was 170; and at Chincoteague for the same period it was 153. The Cape Charles counts usually are higher than Chincoteague's because the number of participants at the Cape averages about 40-50 compared to 20-25 at Chincoteague, and because of the funneling of birds into the southern tip of the Eastern Shore of the Virginia peninsula, and the consequent build-up and concentration at that point where land stops. The "pile-up" of birds at Cape Charles would be expected, as transient birds arriving at that point face the wide mouth of Chesapeake Bay, and stop along the migration route where they can rest and feed before continuing under more favorable weather conditions or whatever.

Many species, particularly waterfowl (Fig. 88) will spend the winter in the area, as they do at Chincoteague.

Fig. 88—A picture out of the past? Not quite. Flocks of pintails like this are still seen occasionally in winter along coastal embayments. In some years, over 5,000 pintails are counted on the one-day Christmas census in the Chincoteague area. A report in *American Birds* indicated that D.F. Abbott and Henry Bielstein estimated 100,000 waterfowl at the Wash Flats area, Chincoteague National Wildlife Refuge on November 16, 1977.

The variety of waterfowl at Chincoteague is enhanced by the freshwater impoundments at the Refuge. Such ponds especially attract dabblers or puddle ducks, the mallard, shoveler, green-winged teal, as well as the whistling swan (Fig. 89), and a few divers such as the lesser scaup and canvasback (Fig. 90). Other areas or habitats covered in the 15-mile count circle include the barrier islands, salt marshes, embayments between the barrier islands and the mainland, and the littoral or immediate offshore zone.

Participants in the Christmas Count assemble the evening before "the big day" to be assigned their parcel of land for censusing. The so-called regulars or persons participating year after year usually return to the same section of marsh, ocean beach, or pinewoods that they know best and can most effectively cover (Fig. 91). The 24-hour affair begins at midnight for a few eager birders who want to make the most of the opportunity to hear the calls of owls, rails, woodcock, and other nighttime sounds.

The most exciting part of a Christmas Count is the spotting of a rare or unusual bird. Many are far off course and beyond their normal range. It is also of much interest to discover a bird that should have passed through on fall migration, but that for some unknown reason has lagged behind. Some of the warblers are known for this, particularly the Nashville, Wilson's, black and white, and black-throated blue, also the white-eyed and solitary vireos. Some of these species should be in the tropics or south Florida at this time of the year.

In my judgment, the most unusual record was that of a common cuckoo (*Cuculus canorus*), a European species, at Cape Charles on the December 1965 Christmas Count. Apparently this was the first sighting of this species in North America. The following note was appended to the published report:

Fig. 89—Six whistling swans and two Canada geese (above) asleep at Chincoteague. Note head of herring gull in front of goose in left foreground.

Fig. 90—Canvasbacks winter in small numbers in Chincoteague Bay and other embayments behind the barrier beaches. Note two birds preparing to dive for food.

Mike Haramis, USFWS

Seen well, all field marks by experienced Englishman Martin Cody, graduate student at Univ. of Pa. Page of convincing details submitted; not listed in A.O.U. Check-List, but an interesting possibility. (Ed.)

A.O.U.Check-List refers to the American Ornithologists' Union *Check-List of North American Birds.* It is not unusual for a seabird or waterfowl species to occasionally wander to the North American Coast, but a songbird species is much less likely to do so.

Some other unusual records were as follows:

- Bar-tailed godwit, whose range is northern Alaska, Siberia, and Northern Europe.
- Chuck-will's-widow (close relative of the whip-poor-will), summer resident of the Delmarva Peninsula that winters mainly in the tropics.
- Bachman's sparrow, a bird of the southern United States well north of its normal range.
- Oregon junco of the North Pacific Coast.
- Lincoln's sparrow, a seldom observed migrant that nests in New England and Canada, and winters in the south. This bird is very shy and difficult to identify at any time because it closely resembles an immature swamp sparrow, a species that is common in the fall, winter, and spring on the Eastern Shore of Virginia.
- Yellow rail, a small secretive bird that winters mainly along the Gulf Coast. This night migrant rarely flies during the day, usually hiding in dense marsh cover.

Another special feature, but one that birders have come to expect when they go on a Christmas Count, is the southern incursion of northern finches. This group is usually well represented by the evening grosbeak, red crossbill (122 in 1969 at Chincoteague), pine siskin, and occasionally a redpoll or pine grosbeak. The greater the food shortage in the northern evergreen forest the greater the number of these coniferous seed-eating species that appear in the Middle At-

Mike Haramis. USFWS

Fig. 91—Greater snow geese passing over ornithologist as he leaves the marsh during a Christmas Bird Count.

lantic States. The red-breasted nuthatch, also a northern coniferous zone bird, is nearly always present. Other specialties are those species that occur in the sand dunes, the Ipswich sparrow, snow bunting, and rarely the Lapland longspur. A few years ago the Ipswich sparrow lost species status and is now considered a subspecies or variety of the much more common Savannah sparrow. However, as noted previously it is usually possible to separate the two in the field—the Ipswich being larger, lighter, and always in the sand dunes. Another northern bird, the purple sandpiper, is usually associated with the ocean jetties.

Always of special interest are those spring and summer backyard and front lawn birds, the robin, gray catbird, brown thrasher (Fig. 92), and the eastern bluebird of our orchards, that leave us in the fall for wintering grounds mainly in the southern states, except for the few that linger along the lower Delmarva coast. In 1969 there were 2,201 robins at Cape Charles; in 1973, 73 gray catbirds at Chincoteague; in 1965, 52 brown thrashers at Chincoteague, and in 1974, 98 bluebirds at Chincoteague.

Some unusually high Christmas Counts of certain species of water birds along the Virginia coast are notable:

Atlantic brant (Chincoteague, 1966)	32,000
Dunlin (Cape Charles, 1972)	18,369
Surf scoter (Cape Charles, 1971)	11,920
Black-bellied plover (Cape Charles, 1973)	1,605
Red-breasted merganser (Cape Charles, 1971)	1,471
Bonapart's gull (Cape Charles, 1976)	1,010
American oystercatcher (Cape Charles, 1974)	684
Common loon (Chincoteague, 1970)	641
Horned grebe (Cape Charles, 1971)	566
Willet (Cape Charles, 1974)	190
Gannet (Cape Charles, 1973)	183
Woodcock (Cape Charles, 1968)	122
Louisiana heron (Cape Charles, 1971)	84

Painting by Louis Agassiz Fuertes, Courtesy USFWS

Fig. 92—Brown thrasher, common spring and summer bird of suburban residential hedgerows, winters in small numbers along the Virginia Coastal Strand. In 1965, there were 52 reported on the one-day Chincoteague Christmas Count.

Some Unusual Bird Records

A number of birds that have strayed far beyond their normal range are reported from the Virginia Coastal Strand each year. Some are **European** or **Asiatic** species that have been observed only once or twice in the area; or some from the **Old World**, like the ruff, curlew sandpiper, and European wigeon have occurred a number of times. There are also a number of oceanic or pelagic species that regularly occur far out at sea opposite the Virginia coast, but occasionally drift in or are blown shoreward by a storm. Some pelagic species like the gannet occur close to shore quite often; others like the red phalarope, skua, and fulmar, occur quite rarely.

Because of the coastal location, many of the unexpected birds are seabirds or shorebirds; however, many are from the south and west that wander to the coast following the nesting season. Most records are in the summer and fall and the majority of the strays are immatures or young of the year.

Bob Hines, USFWS

Fig. 93—The frigate bird inhabits tropical and subtropical seas and coasts. It rarely wanders as far north as the South Carolina coast, and is truly accidental along the Virginia coast.

Herons, egrets, ibises, anhingas, and brown pelicans are **southern** birds especially well known as post-nesting season wanderers. In the summer of 1977, there was a considerable incursion of white ibises into the Middle Atlantic region. These birds probably came from coastal North or South Carolina breeding colonies. Some of the white ibises arrived around the first of July and remained in the same locale until mid-September.

The eastward wandering of certain **western** birds may be due to some extent to the Prevailing Westerlies (winds), or, in the case of a few species, to regular eastward movement that cannot be reasonably explained. An example of the latter is Brewer's blackbird, a species that breeds mainly from the Great Plains westward. A few have extended their breeding range as far east as Indiana. A small flock of Brewer's blackbirds occurs almost every winter in a certain pasture near Bombay Hook National Wildlife Refuge in Delaware. There has to be something traditional about such regularity. Records of Brewer's appear to be rare along the Virginia coast. One was seen there on December 27, 1972, by Paul Sykes. Two or three yellow-headed blackbirds, a western species that has somewhat the same breeding range as Brewer's blackbird, are observed in the Middle Atlantic Coast region each year.

A number of western land birds wander eastward to the coast until they reach the barrier of the ocean. Thus if there is going to be a concentration of strays anywhere, the coast would be the predictable area. Since the coastal section is relatively open and is the principal area frequented by birders, more unusual bird records come from there. A number of new **pelagic** or **oceanic** bird records are due to birds dying at sea and being washed ashore where they are found by beachcombing ornithologists.

New birds are added to a state's list usually on the following basis: a specimen obtained by some means, i.e., trapped by a bird bander or picked up dead on an ocean beach, an identifiable photograph, or sighting at least three different times by competent observers.

Most of the following selected records of rare and unusual birds that have occurred along the Virginia coast in recent years were previously published in *American Birds* (or its predecessor, *Audubon Field Notes*), publication of the National Audubon Society, and in the *Raven*, journal of the Virginia Society of Ornithology—

Pelagic or Oceanic Birds

Magnificent Frigate Bird (also called *Man-O-War Bird*). Observed at Hog Island, July 10, 1972, by T.J. Ayland and A.H. Thompson. The frigate bird is a large seabird of tropical waters, regularly occurring off the Florida Keys and Gulf Coast, south through the West Indies and coast of South America. This awesome looking bird has a long bill, hooked at the end, long pointed wings with a 7-8 foot spread, and a deeply forked tail (Fig. 93). It is often ob-

Fig. 94—The anhinga is a bird of the southern coastal plain swamps and rarely wanders as far north as the Middle Atlantic Coast. One was seen at Chincoteague National Wildlife Refuge on October 7, 1973.

Luther C. Goldman, USFWS

served sailing at great altitudes, from which it may suddenly drop to harass another seabird forcing it to release its newly caught bounty.

Sabine's Gull. Seen near Assateague Island, May 28, 1972, by Paul Dumont. This northern gull breeds in the Arctic from Alaska to Greenland. It is a bird inhabiting cold currents. Many winter off the coast of Peru where there is a cold Antarctic current. Rare in the Atlantic at the latitude of the Virginia coast.

Leach's Petrel. Seen in the Chesapeake Bay Bridge-Tunnel area by R.B. Gordon on January 10, 1971. Although it breeds as near as the coast of Maine, it is rare south of there along the Atlantic coast, wintering mainly in tropical waters near the Equator. Wilson's petrel (Mother Carey's Chicken of the mariner), on the other hand, breeds in the Antarctic region and is frequently seen off the Middle Atlantic Coast.

Arctic Birds

Bar-tailed Godwit. Observed at Chincoteague, December 28, 1973, by Robert Pyle. It nests in Arctic Alaska, Siberia, and northern Europe. The winter range includes the British Isles, Black Sea, Arabia, northwest India, southeast China, and the Philippines south to Australia and New Zealand.

Wheatear. There have been two sightings of this songbird on the Eastern Shore of Virginia. The first was of a bird seen near Townsend on October 3, 1971, reported by

95

Sydney and Dorothy Mitchell. The second was seen in the spring of 1978. The wheatear breeds from northern Europe and parts of the British Isles, and in the Arctic from Greenland to Alaska.

Western Birds

Chestnut-collared Longspur. Observed at Chincoteague Refuge, June 5, 1977, by E.N. Breden, P. Fahey, and R.J. Smith. This species breeds in the northern Great Plains, wintering in the southern plains and Mexico.

Long-billed Curlew. This largest of shorebirds was seen at Cape Charles, December 29, 1969, by H.T. Armistead, et al. Two were also seen along the Virginia coast by J.H. Buckalew in the spring of 1978. The long-billed curlew breeds in the grasslands of the northern Great Plains, wintering in the southwestern states south to Guatemala.

Mountain Plover. This upland shorebird was observed by Claudia Wilds and others at Chincoteague Refuge, October 16, 1976. The mountain plover breeds in the shortgrass prairie of the western plains, wintering in southern Texas, California, and Mexico.

Clay-colored Sparrow. Observed by F.G. Scheider at Assateague, October 11, 1961. This bird of the northern Great Plains winters southward into Mexico.

LeConte's Sparrow. Another Great Plains breeding bird; this sparrow was seen at the Chesapeake Bay Bridge-Tunnel area, November 24, 1970 by D.W. Sonneborn.

LeConte's sparrow winters in the south-central and southeastern states.

Western Kingbird. There are a number of records of the occurrence of this western plains bird along the east coast. One of the more recent records was of a bird seen at Kiptopeke by R.L. Ake on March 9, 1974.

White Pelican. Observed at Chincoteague, August 30, 1971, by J.M. Abbott and others. Breeds in western United States and Canada. There are several nesting colonies on islands in Great Salt Lake. Winters mainly along the Gulf Coast of the United States and the east and west coasts of Mexico.

Southern Birds

Anhinga. Also known as the *water turkey* and *snakebird*, this bird of the swamps of the deep south was seen at Chincoteague Refuge, October 7 and 8, 1973, by E. Liner and B. Sperling (Fig. 94).

Purple Gallinule. This member of the rail family that inhabits southern freshwater marshes, was seen at Chincoteague Refuge, July 28, 1972, by Richard A. Rowlett. There is a nesting record for Maryland and for Delaware. Otherwise it is rare at any time this far north.

Gray Kingbird. In the United States, this subtropical and tropical songbird, a member of the flycatcher family,

Fig. 95—The black rail, secretive bird of salt and brackish marshes.

is found mainly in Florida, with two or three nesting records in coastal Georgia and South Carolina. Richard Rowlett saw one at Chincoteague Refuge on July 7, 1977. This was the first Virginia record of that species.

Other Birds

King Rail. A species that is associated mainly with fresh or slightly brackish marshes, the king rail is seen occasionally along the coastal strand, and up to a half dozen are sometimes reported on the Chincoteague or Cape Charles Christmas Counts. This close to the coast, kings are usually found in a freshwater impoundment or rainwater pool with cattails or some other freshwater

plant, but in June, 1951, Robert E. Stewart saw a mated clapper rail and king rail with brood walking out of a salt marsh at Chincoteague.

Black Rail (Fig. 95). This species may not be so rare as it is hard to find. It is about the size of a sparrow and is one of the most secretive of birds, seldom flying except during migration. It lives more like a mouse in the windblown salt-meadow cordgrass.

John Buckalew, former manager of the Chincoteague National Wildlife Refuge, recalls that in the early days of the Refuge (1940s) where a freshwater impoundment is now located, there was a small colony where they could always be heard at night during the breeding season. Such breeding populations appear to be rare on the Eastern Shore of Virginia today.

In the course of trapping small rodents at Chincoteague, a mammologist of the U.S. National Museum caught a black rail in a mousetrap. There are two records from Christmas Counts at Cape Charles: December 27, 1971, and December 29, 1973. This little rail is a fairly common breeding bird in the salt meadows at Elliott Island in Dorchester County, Maryland. Some breeding birds also occur in the Deal Island area of Somerset County, Maryland. At these places they are sometimes heard, but rarely seen.

In my 50 years' association with Maryland and Virginia birders, I would say that there are few birds that are higher on the list of desiderata than the black rail.

Appendix I

Chincoteague and Cape Charles Christmas Bird Counts
(highest number reported in any one year)

Species	*Chinco-teague	Cape Charles	Species	*Chinco-teague	Cape Charles
common loon	641	125	glossy ibis	32	7
red-throated loon	292	115	mute swan	41	0
red-necked grebe	7	3	whistling swan	1,193	476
horned grebe	2,269	566	Canada goose	7,498	5,575
eared grebe	1	0	Atlantic brant	32,000	8,724
pied-billed grebe	175	78	snow goose	21,779	420
white pelican	1	0	mallard	1,888	1,685
gannet	13	269	black duck	13,400	1,865
great cormorant	1	11	gadwall	770	294
double-crested cormorant	28	21	pintail	5,046	128
great blue heron	303	216	green-winged teal	4,200	199
green heron	3	4	blue-winged teal	9	8
little blue heron	86	51	northern shoveler	1,787	148
cattle egret	2	4	European wigeon	3	1
great egret	215	38	American wigeon	1,037	695
snowy egret	109	55	wood duck	7	14
Louisiana heron	132	106	redhead	225	55
black-crowned night heron	139	95	ring-necked duck	200	516
yellow-crowned night heron	2	2	canvasback	1,450	138
American bittern	24	16	greater scaup	730	51

*Chincoteague 1952-1976   Cape Charles 1965-1976

Note: Data from *Audubon Field Notes* and *American Birds*

Species	*Chinco- teague	Cape Charles
lesser scaup	68	258
common goldeneye	524	308
bufflehead	2,262	5,475
common eider	0	1
king eider	1	0
oldsquaw	2,485	1,046
white-winged scoter	612	299
surf scoter	4,372	11,920
black scoter	16,300	1,208
ruddy duck	633	106
hooded merganser	283	250
common merganser	19	14
red-breasted merganser	511	1,417
turkey vulture	260	300
black vulture	14	18
sharp-shinned hawk	31	56
Cooper's hawk	5	5
red-tailed hawk	36	47
red-shouldered hawk	16	10
rough-legged hawk	4	4
golden eagle	1	1
bald eagle	3	1
harrier (marsh hawk)	81	97
osprey	0	2
peregrine falcon	3	3

Species	*Chinco- teague	Cape Charles
merlin	5	5
American kestrel	93	132
bobwhite	253	238
ring-necked pheasant	2	11
king rail	4	13
clapper rail	159	155
Virginia rail	28	35
sora	3	15
yellow rail	0	1
black rail	0	2
common gallinule	15	9
American coot	1,091	455
American oystercatcher	550	869
semipalmated plover	24	44
killdeer	202	401
piping plover	11	15
American golden plover	1	0
black-bellied plover	985	1,605
marbled godwit	45	110
bar-tailed godwit	1	0
whimbrel	2	11
long-billed curlew	0	1
ruddy turnstone	128	298
American woodcock	21	122
common snipe	66	50

Species	*Chinco-teague	Cape Charles
spotted sandpiper	1	1
willet	22	190
greater yellowlegs	101	181
lesser yellowlegs	71	60
knot	520	18
purple sandpiper	0	7
pectoral sandpiper	1	4
least sandpiper	83	49
dunlin	15,786	19,290
short-billed dowitcher	22	39
long-billed dowitcher	24	3
semipalmated sandpiper	570	457
western sandpiper	1,220	145
sanderling	2,405	1,122
American avocet	18	2
pomarine jaeger	0	2
glaucous gull	1	1
Iceland gull	0	1
great black-backed gull	714	1,328
herring gull	7,610	14,005
ring-billed gull	2,156	5,228
black-headed gull	1	1
laughing gull	2	6
Bonapart's gull	735	1,010
little gull	1	1

Species	*Chinco-teague	Cape Charles
black-legged kittiwake	1	0
Forster's tern	80	105
common tern	8	0
royal tern	2	11
Caspian tern	1	0
black skimmer	7	16
rock dove	80	1,120
mourning dove	651	1,335
common cuckoo	0	1
barn owl	4	5
screech owl	39	60
great horned owl	16	31
barred owl	1	1
long-eared owl	0	1
short-eared owl	31	14
saw-whet owl	3	1
chuck-will's-widow	1	0
belted kingfisher	97	69
common flicker	386	434
pileated woodpecker	11	1
red-bellied woodpecker	78	61
red-headed woodpecker	21	9
yellow-bellied sapsucker	11	10
hairy woodpecker	24	25
downy woodpecker	152	70

Species	*Chinco-teague	Cape Charles	Species	*Chinco-teague	Cape Charles
western kingbird	1	2	hermit thrush	98	59
eastern phoebe	15	13	Swainson's thrush	1	1
horned lark	215	296	eastern bluebird	98	59
tree swallow	2,482	70	blue-gray gnatcatcher	1	2
blue jay	156	102	golden-crowned kinglet	444	216
common crow	11,000	380	ruby-crowned kinglet	226	92
fish crow	5,228	111	water pipit	510	1,414
black-capped chickadee	2	0	cedar waxwing	218	262
Carolina chickadee	356	455	loggerhead shrike	3	9
tufted titmouse	101	51	starling	11,956	8,090
white-breasted nuthatch	10	9	white-eyed vireo	0	1
red-breasted nuthatch	194	114	solitary vireo	0	1
brown-headed nuthatch	215	117	Philadelphia vireo	0	1
brown creeper	79	39	black and white warbler	2	2
house wren	24	51	orange-crowned warbler	4	5
winter wren	42	61	Nashville warbler	0	2
Bewick's wren	0	1	black-throated blue warbler	0	1
Carolina wren	354	489	pine warbler	16	20
marsh wren	58	129	prairie warbler	1	2
sedge wren	30	55	Cape May warbler	1	0
mockingbird	91	176	blackburnian warbler	1	0
gray catbird	88	48	yellow-rumped warbler	11,956	8,090
brown thrasher	52	29	palm warbler	118	487
robin	1,775	2,201	ovenbird	0	1
wood thrush	0	1	northern waterthrush	0	1

Species	*Chinco- teague	Cape Charles
yellowthroat	22	21
yellow-breasted chat	2	6
Wilson's warbler	0	1
house sparrow	810	708
eastern meadowlark	1,005	1,078
yellow-headed blackbird	1	1
red-winged blackbird	47,402	46,176
northern oriole	1	1
rusty blackbird	192	66
Brewer's blackbird	1	1
boat-tailed grackle	7,384	2,496
common grackle	96,513	73,197
brown-headed cowbird	3,678	2,793
cardinal	427	512
dickcissel	0	1
evening grosbeak	335	476
indigo bunting	1	0
purple finch	71	36
house finch	102	130
common redpoll	9	2
pine siskin	204	677
American goldfinch	707	991
red crossbill	122	103
white-winged crossbill	0	4
rufous-sided towhee	205	283

Species	*Chinco- teague	Cape Charles
Ipswich sparrow	6	11
Savannah sparrow	435	839
grasshopper sparrow	1	2
Henslow's sparrow	1	0
sharp-tailed sparrow	121	213
seaside sparrow	26	165
vesper sparrow	53	70
Bachman's sparrow	0	1
dark-eyed junco	463	269
Oregon junco	1	1
tree sparrow	19	30
chipping sparrow	35	59
field sparrow	431	404
white-crowned sparrow	11	27
white-throated sparrow	2,747	3,015
fox sparrow	67	317
Lincoln's sparrow	1	5
swamp sparrow	820	1,025
song sparrow	1,095	1,472
Lapland longspur	25	7
snow bunting	354	185

anhinga (*Anhinga anhinga*)

auks (*Alcidae*)

avocet, American (*Recurvirostra americana*)

bittern, American (*Botaurus lentiginosus*)

blackbird, Brewer's (*Euphagus cyanocephalus*)

red-winged (*Agelaius phoeniceus*)

rusty (*Euphagus carolinus*)

yellow-headed (*Xanthocephalus xanthocephalus*)

bluebird, eastern (*Sialia sialis*)

bobwhite (*Colinus virginianus*)

brant, Atlantic (*Branta bernicla*)

bufflehead (*Bucephala albeola*)

bunting, indigo (*Passerina cyanea*)

snow (*Plectrophenax nivalis*)

canvasback (*Aythya valisineria*)

cardinal (*Cardinalis cardinalis*)

catbird, gray (*Dumetella carolinensis*)

chat, yellow-breasted (*Icteria virens*)

chickadee, black-capped (*Parus atricapillus*)

Carolina (*Parus carolinensis*)

chuck-will's-widow (*Caprimulgus carolinensis*)

cowbird, brown-headed (*Molothrus ater*)

coot, American (*Fulica americana*)

cormorant, double-crested (*Phalacrocorax auritus*)

great (*Phalacrocorax carbo*)

creeper, brown (*Certhia familiaris*)

crossbill, red (*Loxia curvirostra*)

white-winged (*Loxia leucoptera*)

crow, common (*Corvus brachyrhynchos*)

fish (*Corvus ossifragus*)

cuckoo, common (*Cuculus canorus*)

curlew, Eskimo (*Numenius borealis*)

long-billed (*Numenius americanus*)

dickcissel (*Spiza americana*)

dove, mourning (*Zenaida macroura*)

rock (*Columbia livia*)

dovekie (*Plautus alle*)

dowitcher, long-billed (*Limnodromus scolopaceus*)

short-billed (*Limnodromus griseus*)

duck, Bahama (*Anas bahamensis*)

black (*Anas rubripes*)

fulvous tree or fulvous whistling (*Dendrocynga bicolor*)

harlequin (*Histrionicus histrionicus*)

ring-necked (*Aythya collaris*)

ruddy (*Oxyura jamaicensis*)

wood (*Aix sponsa*)

dunlin (*Erolia alpina*)

eagle, bald (*Haliaeetus leucocephalus*)

golden (*Aquila chrysaetos*)

egret, cattle (*Bubulcus ibis*)

great (*Casmerodius albus*)

snowy (*Egretta thula*)

eider, common (*Somateria mollissima*)

king (*Somateria spectabilis*)

falcon, peregrine (*Falco peregrinus*)

finch, house (*Carpodacus mexicanus*)

purple (*Carpodacus purpureus*)

flicker, common (*Colaptes auratus*)

flycatcher, great crested (*Myiarchus crinitus*)

frigate bird, magnificent (*Fregata magnificens*)

fulmar (*Fulmarus glacialis*)

gadwall (*Anas strepera*)

gallinule, common (*Gallinula chloropus*)

gannet (*Morus bassanus*)

gnatcatcher, blue-gray (*Polioptela caerulea*)

godwit, bar-tailed (*Limosa lapponica*)

Hudsonian (*Limosa haemastica*)

marbled (*Limosa fedoa*)

goldeneye, common (*Bucephala clangula*)
goldfinch, American (*Spinus tristis*)
goose, Canada (*Branta canadensis*)
    greater snow (*Anser caerulescens atlanticus*)
    lesser snow (*Anser caerulescens caerulescens*)
grackle, boat-tailed (*Quiscalus major*)
    common (*Quiscalus quiscula*)
grebe, eared (*Podiceps caspicus*)
    horned (*Podiceps auritus*)
    pied-billed (*Podilymbus podiceps*)
    red-necked (*Podiceps grisegena*)
grosbeak, black-headed (*Pheucticus melanocephalus*)
    evening (*Hesperiphona vespertina*)
    pine (*Pinicola eneucleator*)
guillemot, black (*Cepphus grylle*)
gull, black-headed (*Larus ridibundus*)
    Bonapart's (*Larus philadelphia*)
    glaucous (*Larus hyperboreus*)
    great black-backed (*Larus marinus*)
    herring (*Larus argentatus*)
    Iceland (*Larus glaucoides*)
    laughing (*Larus atricilla*)
    little (*Larus minutus*)
    ring-billed (*Larus delawarensis*)
    Sabine's (*Xema sabini*)

harrier or marsh hawk (*Circus cyaneus*)
hawk, broad-winged (*Buteo platypterus*)
    Cooper's (*Accipiter cooperii*)

red-shouldered (*Buteo lineatus*)
    red-tailed (*Buteo jamaicensis*)
    rough-legged (*Buteo lagopus*)
    sharp-shinned (*Accipiter striatus*)
heron, black-crowned night (*Nycticorax nycticorax*)
    great blue (*Ardea herodias*)
    green (*Butorides virescens*)
    little blue (*Florida caerulea*)
    Louisiana (*Hydranassa tricolor*)
    yellow-crowned night (*Nyctanassa violacea*)
hummingbird, ruby-throated (*Archilochus colubris*)

ibis, glossy (*Plegadis falcinellus*)
    white (*Eudocimus albus*)

jaeger, long-tailed (*Stercorarius longicaudus*)
    parasitic (*Stercorarius parasiticus*)
    pomarine (*Stercorarius pomarinus*)
jay, blue (*Cyanocitta cristata*)
junco, dark-eyed (*Junco hyemalis*)
    Oregon (*Junco oreganus*)

kestrel (*Falco sparvarius*)
killdeer (*Charadrius vociferus*)
kingbird, eastern (*Tyrannus tyrannus*)
    gray (*Tyrannus dominicensis*)
    western (*Tyrannus verticalis*)
kingfisher, belted (*Megaceryle alcyon*)

kinglet, golden-crowned (*Regulus satrapa*)
    ruby-crowned (*Regulus calendula*)
kittiwake, black-legged (*Rissa tridactyla*)
knot (*Calidris canutus*)

lark, horned (*Eremophila alpestris*)
longspur, chestnut-colored (*Calcarius ornatus*)
    Lapland (*Calcarius lapponicus*)
    Smith's (*Calcarius pictus*)
loon, common (*Gavia immer*)
    red-throated (*Gavia stellata*)

mallard (*Anas platyrhynchos*)
meadowlark, eastern (*Sturnella magna*)
merganser, common (*Mergus merganser*)
    hooded (*Mergus cucullatus*)
    red-breasted (*Mergus serrator*)
merlin (*Falco columbarius*)
mockingbird (*Mimus polyglottos*)
murre, thick-billed (*Uria lomvia*)

nighthawk, common (*Chordeiles minor*)
nuthatch, brown-headed (*Sitta pusilla*)
    red-breasted (*Sitta canadensis*)
    white-breasted (*Sitta carolinensis*)

oldsquaw (*Clangula hyemalis*)
oriole, northern or Baltimore (*Icterus galbula galbula*)

northern or Bullock's (*Icterus galbula
    bullockii*)

osprey (*Pandion haliaetus*)
ovenbird (*Seiurus aurocapillus*)
owl, barn (*Tyto alba*)
    barred (*Strix varia*)
    great horned (*Bubo virginianus*)
    long-eared (*Asio otus*)
    saw-whet (*Aegolius acadicus*)
    screech (*Otus asio*)
    short-eared (*Asio flammeus*)
oystercatcher, American (*Haematopus palliatus*)
    black (*Haematopus bachmani*)

pelican, brown (*Pelecanus occidentalis*)
    white (*Pelecanus erythrorhynchos*)
petrel, Leach's (*Oceanodroma leucorhoa*)
    Wilson's (*Oceanites oceanicus*)
pewee, eastern wood (*Contopus virens*)
phalarope, red (*Phalaropus fulicarius*)
pheasant, ring-necked (*Phasianus colchicus*)
phoebe, eastern (*Sayornis phoebe*)
pintail (*Anas acuta*)
pipit, water (*Anthus spinoletta*)
plover, American golden (*Pluvialis dominica*)
    black-bellied (*Squatarola squatarola*)
    mountain (*Eupoda montana*)
    piping (*Charadrius melodus*)

semipalmated (*Charadrius semipalmatus*)
    Wilson's (*Charadrius wilsonia*)
puffin, common (*Fratercula arctica*)

rail, black (*Laterallus jamaicensis*)
    clapper (*Rallus longirostris*)
    king (*Rallus elegans*)
    Virginia (*Rallus limicola*)
    yellow (*Coturnicops novaboracensis*)
razorbill (*Alca torda*)
redhead (*Aythya americana*)
redstart, American (*Setophaga ruticilla*)
redpoll, common (*Acanthis flammea*)
robin (*Turdus migratorius*)
ruff (*Philomachus pugnax*)

sanderling (*Crocethia alba*)
sandpiper, Baird's (*Erolia bairdii*)
    curlew (*Erolia ferruginea*)
    least (*Erolia minutilla*)
    pectoral (*Erolia melanotos*)
    purple (*Erolia maritima*)
    semipalmated (*Calidris pusilla*)
    spotted (*Actitis macularia*)
    stilt (*Micropalama himantopus*)
    upland (*Bartramia longicauda*)
    western (*Ereunetes mauri*)
    white-rumped (*Calidris fuscicollis*)
sapsucker, yellow-bellied (*Sphyrapicus varius*)

scaup, greater (*Aythya marila*)
    lesser (*Aythya affinis*)
scoter, black (*Melanitta nigra*)
    surf (*Melanitta perspicillata*)
    white-winged (*Melanitta fusca*)
shearwater, Audubon's (*Puffinus lherminieri*)
    Cory's (*Puffinus diomedea*)
    greater (*Puffinus gravis*)
    sooty (*Puffinus griseus*)
shrike, loggerhead (*Lanius ludovicianus*)
shoveler, northern (*Anas clypeata*)
siskin, pine (*Spinus pinus*)
skimmer, black (*Rynchops niger*)
snipe, common (*Capella gallinago*)
sora (*Porzana carolina*)
sparrow, Bachman's (*Aimophila aestivalis*)
    chipping (*Spizella passerina*)
    clay-colored (*Spizella pallida*)
    field (*Spizella pusilla*)
    fox (*Passerella iliaca*)
    grasshopper (*Ammodramus savannarum*)
    Henslow's (*Passerherbulus henslowii*)
    house (*Passer domesticus*)
    Ipswich (*Passerculus sandwichensis
        principes*)
    LeConte's (*Passerherbulus caudacutus*)
    Lincoln's (*Melospiza lincolnii*)
    savannah (*Passerculus sandwichensis*)
    seaside (*Ammospiza maritima*)

sharp-tailed (*Ammospiza caudacuta*)
song (*Melospiza melodia*)
swamp (*Melospiza georgiana*)
tree (*Spizella arborea*)
vesper (*Pooecetes gramineus*)
white-crowned (*Zonotrichia leucophrys*)
white-throated (*Zonotrichia albicollis*)
starling (*Sturnus vulgaris*)
stilt, black-necked (*Himantopus mexicanus*)
swallow, barn (*Hirundo rustica*)
tree (*Iridoprocne bicolor*)
swan, mute (*Cygnus olor*)
whistling (*Olar columbianus*)

tanager, summer (*Piranga rubra*)
teal, blue-winged (*Anas discors*)
green-winged (*Anas crecca*)
tern, black (*Chlidonias niger*)
Caspian (*Hydroprogne caspia*)
common (*Sterna hirundo*)
Forster's (*Sterna forsteri*)
gull-billed (*Gelochelidon nilotica*)
least or little (*Sterna albifrons*)
roseate (*Sterna dougallii*)
royal (*Thalasseus maximus*)
sandwich (*Thalasseus sandvicensis*)

thrasher, brown (*Toxostoma rufum*)
thrush, gray-cheeked (*Hyloccichla minima*)
hermit (*Catharus guttatus*)
Swainson's (*Catharus ustalatus*)
wood (*Hylocichla mustelina*)
titmouse, tufted (*Parus bicolor*)
towhee, rufous-sided (*Pipilo erythrophthalmus*)
turnstone, ruddy (*Arenaria interpres*)

vireo, Philadelphia (*Vireo philadelphicus*)
red-eyed (*Vireo olivaceus*)
solitary (*Vireo solitarius*)
white-eyed (*Vireo griseus*)
vulture, black (*Coragyps atratus*)
turkey (*Cathartes aura*)

warbler, black and white (*Mniotilta varia*)
blackburnian (*Dendroica fusca*)
blackpoll (*Dendroica striata*)
black-throated blue (*Dendroica caerulescens*)
Cape May (*Dendroica tigrina*)
Nashville (*Vermivora ruficapilla*)
orange-crowned (*Vermivora celata*)
palm (*Dendroica palmarum*)
pine (*Dendroica pinus*)
prairie (*Dendroica discolor*)

Wilson's (*Wilsonia pusilla*)
yellow (*Dendroica petechia*)
yellow-rumped (*Dendroica coronata*)
waterthrush, northern (*Seiurus noveboracensis*)
waxwing, cedar (*Bombycilla cedrorum*)
wheatear (*Oenanthe oenanthe*)
whimbrel (*Numenius phaeopus*)
wigeon, American (*Anas americana*)
European (*Anas penelope*)
willet (*Catoptrophorus semipalmatus*)
woodcock, American (*Philohela minor*)
woodpecker, downy (*Picoides pubescens*)
hairy (*Picoides villosus*)
pileated (*Dendrocopus pileatus*)
red-bellied (*Melanerpes carolinus*)
red-headed (*Melanerpes erythrocephalus*)
wren, Bewick's (*Thryomanes bewickii*)
Carolina (*Thryothorus ludovicianus*)
house (*Troglodytes aedon*)
marsh (*Cistothorus palustris*)
sedge (*Cistothorus platensis*)
winter (*Troglodytes troglodytes*)

yellowlegs, greater (*Tringa melanoleuca*)
lesser (*Tringa flavipes*)
yellowthroat, common (*Geothlypis trichas*)

Common and Scientific Names of Other Animals

anchovy, bay (*Anchoa mitchilli*)
beetles (*Coleoptera*)
bluefish (*Pomotomus saltatrix*)
clam, hard-shelled (*Mercenaria pallaitus*)
crab, blue (*Callinectes sapidus*)
    fiddler (*Uca* sp.)
    mud (*Neopanope texana-say*)
    spider (*Libinia emarginata*)

crayfish (*Cambarus* sp.)
killifish (*Fundulus* sp.)
mouse, field (*Microtus pennsylvanicus*)
mullet (*Mugil* sp.)
mussel, ribbed (*Modiolus demissus*)
sandbug (*Emerita talpoida*)
shrimp (*Crago* sp.)
    fairy (*Lepidurus glacialis*)

silversides (*Menidia* sp.)
spot (*Leiostomus zanthurus*)
snail, mud (*Nassarius obsoletus*)
    periwinkle (*Littorina* sp.)
terrapin, diamondback (*Malaclemys terrapin terrapin*)

Common and Scientific Names of Plants

bulrush, salt-marsh (*Scirpus robustus*)
cattail (*Typha* sp.)
cedar, red (*Juniperus virginiana*)
cordgrass, salt-marsh (*Spartina alterniflora*)
eelgrass (*Zostera marina*)
grass, salt-meadow (*Spartina patens*)
high-tide bush (*Iva frutescens*)

holly, American (*Ilex opaca*)
lettuce, sea (*Ulva lactuca*)
moss, Spanish (*Tillandsia usneoides*)
myrtle, wax (*Myrica cerifera*)
needlerush (*Juncus roemarianus*)
oak, live (*Quercus virginiana*)
    water (*Quercus nigra*)

pine, loblolly (*Pinus taeda*)
salt grass (*Distichlis spicata*)
spike rush (*Eleocharis* sp.)
three-square, common (*Scirpus americana*)
    Olney (*Scirpus olneyi*)
widgeon grass (*Ruppia maritima*)

Bibliography

(1) Chapman, F.M., 1908. *Camps and cruises of an ornithologist*. D Appleton and Co., New York. 432 p.

(2) Shiras, G., 3rd, 1936. *Hunting wild life with camera and flashlight*. National Geographic Society. Two vols. Washington, D.C. 454 p.

(3) Rowlett, R.A., 1975. First records of Atlantic puffin and yellow-nosed albatross off Maryland. *Maryland Birdlife*, 31:51-56.

(4) Palmer, R.S. (editor), 1976. *Handbook of North American birds*. Vol. 2. Yale University Press, New Haven, Conn. 521 p.

(5) Bellrose, F.C., 1976. *Ducks, geese and swans of North America*. Wildlife Management Institute and Illinois Natural History Survey. Stackpole Books, Harrisburg, Pa. 544 p.

(6) Cottam, C., 1939. *Food habits of North American diving ducks*. U.S. Department of Agriculture, Technical Bulletin No. 643.

(7) Vaughn, C.R., 1971. High loon numbers. *Raven*, 42:52.

(8) Palmer, R.S. (editor), 1962. *Handbook of North American birds*. Vol. 1. Yale University Press, New Haven, Conn. 567 p.

(9) Ake, R.L., and F.R. Scott, 1976. Ki:tiwakes, porpoises and petrels. *Raven*, 47:48.

(10) Murray, J.J., 1957. Major recent changes in Virginia's avifauna. *Raven*, 28:48-52.

(11) Murray, J.J., 1952. *A Check-list of the birds of Virginia*. Virginia Society of Ornithology. 113 p.

(12) Murray, J.J., 1937. June days on Cobb's Island. *Raven*, 8:39-43.

(13) Byrd, M.A., G. Seek, and B. Smith, 1971. Late clapper rail nests. *Raven*, 42:68.

(14) Stewart, R.E., and B. Meanley, 1960. Clutch size of the clapper rail. *Auk*, 77:221-222.

(15) Mangold, R.E., 1974. Clapper rail studies (final report). *Research on shore and upland migratory birds in New Jersey*. Division of Fish, Game, and Shellfishes. Trenton, N.J. 17 p.

(16) Pettingill, O.S., Jr., 1938. Intelligent behavior in the clapper rail. *Auk*, 55:411-415.

(17) Stewart, R.E., 1952. Clapper rail studies. In Aldrich, J.W., et al. *Investigations of woodcock, snipe, and rails in 1951*. U.S. Fish and Wildlife Service, Special Scientific Report-Wildlife. No. 65. 208 p.

(18) Stewart, R.E., 1954. Migratory movements of the northern clapper rail. *Bird-Banding*, 25:1-5.

(19) Adams, D.A., and T.L. Quay, 1958. Ecology of the clapper rail in southeastern North Carolina. *Journal of Wildlife Management*, 22:149-156.

(20) Howell, A.B., 1911. A comparative study of Cobb's Island, Va. *Auk*, 28:449-453.

(21) Sprunt, A., Jr., and E.B. Chamberlain, 1949. *South Carolina bird life*. Contributions from the Charleston Museum:XI. University of South Carolina Press, Columbia, S.C. 585 p.

(22) Kleen, V., 1965. Banding highlights in Maryland. *Maryland Bird-life*, 21:17-20.

(23) Bent, A.C., 1921. *Life histories of North American gulls and terns*. U.S. National Museum Bulletin 113. Smithsonian Institution, Washington, D.C. 345 p.

(24) Erwin, R.M., 1977. Black skimmer breeding ecology and behavior. *Auk*, 94:709-717.

(25) Byrd, M.A., et al, 1976. Middle Atlantic Coast region (F.R. Scott, editor). *American Birds*. National Audubon Society, New York, N.Y. 940-941.

(26) Pettingill, O.S., Jr., 1937. Behavior of black skimmers at Cardwell Island, Virginia. *Auk*, 54:237-244.

(27) Tomkins, I.R., 1951. Method of feeding of the black skimmer *Rynchops niger*. *Auk*, 68:236-239.

(28) Zusi, R.L., 1959. Fishing rates in black skimmers. *Condor*, 61:298.

(29) Scott, F.R., 1968. Middle Atlantic Coast region. *American Birds*. National Audubon Society, New York, N.Y. 22:20.

(30) Stewart, R.E., and C.S. Robbins, 1958. *Birds of Maryland and the District of Columbia*. North American Fauna. No. 62. Fish and Wildlife Service, U.S. Department of the Interior. 401 p.

(31) Buckley, P.A., and F.G. Buckley, 1977. Hexagonal packing of royal tern nests. *Auk*, 94:36-43.

(32) Van Velzen, W.T., 1968. The status and dispersal of Virginia royal terns. *Raven*, 39:55-60.

(33) Van Velzen, W.T., and R.D. Benedict, 1972. Recoveries of royal terns banded in Virginia. Part 1. The Caribbean. *Raven*, 43:39-41.

(34) Tomkins, I.R., 1954. Life history notes on the American oyster-catcher. *Oriole*, 19:37-45.

(35) Tomkins, I.R., 1947. The oyster-catcher of the Atlantic Coast of North America and its relation to oysters. *Wilson Bulletin*, 59:204-208.

(36) Baldwin, W.P., 1947. Clam catches oyster-catcher. *Auk*, 63:589.

(37) Frohring, P.C., and R.A. Beck, 1978. First breeding record of the white ibis (*Eudocimus albus*) in Virginia. *American Birds*, 32:126-128.

(38) Valentine, J.M., Jr., 1958. The cattle egret at Chincoteague, Virginia. *Raven*, 29:68-96.

(39) Williams, B., 1975. Growth rate and nesting aspects for the glossy ibis in Virginia. *Raven*, 46:35-51.

(40) Bailey, H.B., 1876. Notes on birds found breeding on Cobb's Island, Va. between May 25th and May 29th, 1875. *Bulletin of the Nuttal Ornithological Club*, 1:24-28.

(41) Meanley, B., 1943. The red-cockaded woodpecker breeding in Maryland. *Auk*, 60:105.

(42) Ward, F.P., and R.B. Berry, 1972. Autumn migration of peregrine falcons on Assateague Island, Maryland, 1970-1971. *Journal of Wildlife Management*, 36:484-492.

(43) Stobo, W.T., and I.A. McLarin, 1975. *The Ipswich sparrow*. Nova Scotia Institute of Science. Halifax, N.S. 105 p.

Index